Advance Praise for *People of the Way*

Just once in a while, you come across a truly great book. The type of book that makes you look at the world in an entirely different way. Dwight Zscheile has written just such a book. He is on top of the literature; he challenges the conventional wisdom; he lives comfortably in the fields of the social sciences and theology; and he sees a deeply creative way forward. *People of the Way* is a work of sheer genius, an absolutely essential addition to the library of anyone seriously concerned about the future of the Episcopal Church. I cannot recommend it more highly.

Ian Markham
President and Dean, Virginia Theological Seminary

Identifying the church as a community of promise and participation, Dwight Zscheile takes a clear-eyed look at the Episcopal Church today and traces the history and the contemporary context that present us with such significant challenges. Without glossing over any mistakes or foolishness, Zscheile retrieves moments, ideas, and traditions that open up a way forward for the church at a time when pronouncements of doom abound. What's laid out here is no quick, technical fix—as if saying "mission" will make it all better—but a call for comprehensive renewal, joining the church's outward-reaching activities with its fundamental spirituality and theology.

It is the interaction of these elements that makes the turn to mission such strong, compelling Good News. I would like to see every congregation and faith community and every church leader get a copy of this book and recognize the many possibilities that God is placing before us today.

Ellen K. Wondra
Editor, Anglican Theological Review

The Episcopal Church finds itself in a new and challenging situation today that we cannot understand without knowing where we have been. As a historian, and a bishop, I find *People of the Way to* be just the volume we need at this moment. It is a serious book that grapples with Episcopal identity in a changing world. It takes the conversation about the church's life to a deeper level of exploring our roots, and it calls us to carry the best of our past into a new future grounded in God's mission. At the same time, *People of the Way* is very accessible and written for widespread use. Rich with stories, as well as theological insights, People of the Way will help my diocese live into a more hopeful tomorrow.

The Rt. Rev. R. William Franklin
Bishop, Diocese of Western New York

When Dwight Zscheile observes that there has been "a striking reluctance among Episcopalians to talk about God," he puts his finger on a critical phenomenon, to which he forcefully responds by offering a recapitulation of the gospel for the twenty-first century. His call for the church to reclaim its identity as centered in an authentic Christian faith is especially timely, contributing to an emerging re-awakening to the centrality of a "robust practice of discipleship" as the *sine qua non* of congregational vitality.

Joseph Britton
President and Dean, Berkeley Divinity School at Yale

People of the Way is a challenging and hope-filled catalyst for fresh conversations and innovations in the way Episcopalians understand and live out God's mission in this generation. Clergy and lay leaders will find transforming insights and creative next steps to explore as they reflect together on the accessible wisdom found here. This book opens our eyes and hearts to God's urgent invitation to embrace a new quality of discipleship and hospitality, grounded in our unique tradition and lived out in our rapidly changing society. I long for this book to be read, prayed, discussed and acted on in every congregation and community.

The Rt. Rev. Gordon Scruton
Bishop, Diocese of Western Massachusetts

Dwight Zscheile gives us more than a book; this is an insightful, honest and straightforward invitation to join a conversation that pays attention to our changing world. Churches everywhere are reassessing their mission and future in light of diminishing attendance and the reality that they no longer reflect their neighborhood. They need this book.

Anthony Guillen
Missioner for Latino/a Ministries, The Episcopal Church Center

In this compelling work, Dwight Zscheile clearly recognizes the centrality of mission and identity. He focuses on mission as central to spiritual health, particularly seeking God's mission as God intends. He challenges us to use the historic tools of Anglicanism under a much higher vision than maintaining or even shoring up the church.

The Rt. Rev. Claude E. Payne
Bishop, Diocese of Texas (Ret.)

PEOPLE *of the* WAY
Renewing Episcopal Identity

PEOPLE *of the* WAY

Renewing Episcopal Identity

DWIGHT J. ZSCHEILE

Morehouse Publishing
NEW YORK · HARRISBURG · DENVER

Unless otherwise noted, the Scripture quotations contained herein are from the New Revised Standard Version Bible, copyright © 1989 by the Division of Christian Education of the National Council of Churches of Christ in the U.S.A. Used by permission. All rights reserved.

Morehouse Publishing, 4775 Linglestown Road, Harrisburg, PA 17112
Morehouse Publishing, 445 Fifth Avenue, New York, NY 10016
Morehouse Publishing is an imprint of Church Publishing Incorporated.
www.churchpublishing.org

Cover design by Laurie Klein Westhafer
Typeset by Beth Oberholtzer

Library of Congress Cataloging-in-Publication Data

Zscheile, Dwight J., 1973-
    People of the way : renewing Episcopal identity / Dwight J. Zscheile.
    p.   cm.
    Includes bibliographical references (p.   ).
    ISBN 978-0-8192-2090-5 (pbk. : alk. paper) — ISBN 978-0-8192-2091-2 (ebook) 1. Episcopal Church. 2. Identification (Religion) I. Title.
 BX5930.3.Z73   2012
 283'.7309051—dc23

                                                        2011051750

Printed in the United States of America

10 9 8 7 6 5 4 3

For Blair, partner in life and ministry,
and for Luke, that he may
continue to bring good news
to those around him.

Contents

Once upon a time the Episcopal Church in the United States was safe and secure in its identity and place in both American societal and religious establishment.[1] Episcopalians knew who they were—who we were. Our self-impression was that, although numerically relatively small as a Christian denomination, we occupied a place of social, political, and religious privilege in the United States. Of course, our good manners and impeccable taste meant that we would never admit publicly that we enjoyed such power and prestige. Still, one only had to count the number of United States presidents, members of Congress, and moguls in business and industry who were Episcopalians to be reassured of our place in American society. This self-understanding of the Episcopal Church, however, all too often neglected significant segments of the church that did not fit the caricature of the self-assured, established, "mainline" White Anglo-Saxon Protestant (WASP) church. African-American congregations, small rural congregations, communities on the Western frontier and among First Nations peoples were often invisible to those who rested in the dominant presupposition of what the Episcopal Church was, or was supposed to be.

For the majority of the twentieth century, the Episcopal Church thus rallied around a national church ideal. The mission of "the national church" was to be a *de facto*, rather than *de jure*, established church for America. Through good schools, good hospitals, and right-ordered worship, the Episcopal Church would spread the richness of Anglican tradition and the riches of democracy and capitalism at home in our urban centers, on the Western frontier, and in missionary outposts in Asia, Latin America, the Caribbean, and parts of Africa. Thus in 1919 the church's separate work in missions, education, and social service came together in a new corporate, centralized programmatic expression under the auspices of a new structure called the National Council led by an elected Presiding Bishop and funded through a diocesan assessment scheme. For over half a century, the National Council and its corporate organization, the Domestic and Foreign Missionary Society, vigorously pursued a program of church extension and robust service to the least and the lost in the best sense of the Social Gospel. Bolstered by the baby boom and economic growth of the post–World War II era, the Episcopal Church grew both numerically and in its confidence as the church for the booming suburbs and emerging nations around the world.

Then something happened. Beginning in the mid-1960s, the self-security of the Episcopal Church as "the national church" began to ebb away in the face of urban unrest, the civil rights movement, and the rise of new nation states in what were Anglo-American colonies. In the wake of the 1969 General Convention Special Program (GCSP) on the United States front, and the vision of Mutual Responsibility and Interdependence in the Body of Christ advanced by the 1963 worldwide Anglican Congress in an increasing postcolonial Anglican Communion, the assumptions and modus operandi of the national church ideal were seriously called into question. Faced with a decreasing shortage of funds, the staff at the Episcopal Church Center in New York, the corporate center for "the national church," was cut abruptly in 1970 from 204 persons to 110. And over the last four decades the centralized program of the Domestic and Foreign Missionary Society has continued to decline as the days of glory for "the national church" have faded away.

Today the glory and grandeur of the Episcopal Church exists primarily in the minds of those who remember the glory days of the mid–twentieth century. Over the last five decades the number of Episcopalians has declined from a high of 3,615,643 baptized members in 1965 to at the present time fewer than two million members—the first time church membership has fallen below two million since 1935.[2] Seemingly innumerable congregations are struggling with declining membership while precariously eating away at their endowments in order to maintain buildings and programs that serve increasingly fewer and fewer people. The loss of the national church ideal has resulted in a crisis of identity for the Episcopal Church. It is a cruel irony that the icon of the national church ideal, namely the Washington National Cathedral, has recently been shaken both figuratively and literally to its foundations with profound economic decline leading to huge cuts in staff and the crumbling of its stonework by the earthquake of August 2011.

Is there any hope for this once privileged and powerful church encountering the new realities of the twenty-first century?

There indeed is! This book presents a vision by which the Episcopal Church can find a new way forward in the twenty-first century. *People of the Way* argues that in service to God's mission of restoration and reconciliation, Episcopalians can discover new meaning, find a new identity, and experience new life and growth.

This work does not shy away from the hard questions: "What does it mean to be a disciple in today's world? What does it mean to be a church member? Are they the same thing? How does the shape of life in the Episcopal Church foster depth and commitment to the way of Christ, and how does it undermine it? What does it mean to be the body of Christ in an increasingly post-Christian America? Who are we as Episcopalians and what are we here for?"[3]

To answer these questions, Dwight Zscheile draws on what is increasingly becoming known as "missional church" and "emerging church" thinking and literature. Zscheile is one of the foremost up and coming missiologists (scholars of Christian mission) in the Episcopal Church. As a young academic and priest who has come to Anglicanism and the Episcopal Church by choice as an adult, Zscheile has a unique and refreshing perspective on the vocation of the Episcopal Church. He argues that putting God's mission first reorients the life of the Episcopal Church and frees it from the confines of the past. The way forward is in God's restoring and reconciling action in and for the world through Jesus Christ by the power of the Holy Spirit.

This book thus invites us to join God in God's mission, to be people of the Jesus Way. It is a twenty-first-century apologetic, in the best sense of the word, for a Christian community that is centered in the Eucharist, empowered for service to God's mission through baptism, and open and responsive to the enculturated realities of a twenty-first-century church in which differences are seen as generative and not problematic. Drawing on contemporary understandings of network organizational theory, Zscheile offers to local Eucharistic communities, to dioceses, and to the general Episcopal Church a vision of what a church organized around and committed to the mission of God might look like. It is a vision of hope, possibility, and new life. It is the way forward in Jesus.

By asking first: What is God up to in our various contexts? and then following with: And what kind of church does God need to serve what God is up to? Zscheile gives us a handbook for a church dedicated to, and finding its identity in, the mission of God. Its accessible language and helpful questions concluding each chapter make it useful for lay and ordained leaders alike. This is the book I have been waiting for. It will help me and the Christian sisters and brothers I am blessed to work alongside in the Episcopal Diocese of Connecticut to become more faithful people of the Way: the Jesus Way, the mission of God Way!

Ian T. Douglas

Acknowledgments

This book is the product of listening and learning from many voices across the church, especially at the grass roots. I want to begin by thanking two congregations in whose midst I have been blessed to serve and who have shaped my imagination for the possibilities of ministry in the twenty-first century—St. Matthew's Episcopal Church in St. Paul, Minnesota, and St. David's Episcopal Church in Ashburn, Virginia. Several dozen members of St. Matthew's read and discussed a draft of this book together, and it is better because of their wisdom.

I am grateful for my mentors and colleagues in the missional church conversation from whom I continue to learn, especially Mark Lau Branson, Patrick Keifert, Alan Roxburgh, Gary Simpson, Jannie Swart, and Craig Van Gelder. A number of leaders around the Episcopal Church were gracious enough to read and respond to drafts of this book—among them Mariann Budde, Ian Douglas, Randy Ferebee, Bill Franklin, Duncan Gray, Tim Hodapp, Rick Lord, Daniel Pearson, Allison Read, Nathan Speck-Ewer, and Gordon Scruton. They have helped improve this work significantly, though I take responsibility for any remaining errors. Francie Hills and Tom McAlpine generously shared rich stories from their congregations.

The dean and faculty of Luther Seminary afforded me a very helpful writing leave to complete this project. Stephanie Spellers, my editor at Church Publishing, has been a source of wisdom and encouragement along the way. Finally, I express my deep appreciation for my wife, Blair Pogue, an astute practitioner of missional leadership, and for the faith, energy, and hopefulness of our son, Luke. May he always know God's love in Christ through the embrace of a vibrant church, and may he help share that love in his own life.

Introduction

Let me begin with the story of a boy. He grew up in a secular home—an environment increasingly common for Americans today. Even though there was enough residual Christianity in his family for him to be baptized as an infant, the story of Jesus had long ceased to shape his family's life. He spent his childhood and adolescence in California, where the church has never been well established. This boy inhabited a narrative that dominates American life today—that you are what you earn or achieve, that identity must be cobbled together from a wide array of shifting possibilities, that you must work incessantly at securing meaning and community because these things are not given. Amidst competition, consumerism, anxiety, and opportunity, life is what you make of it, largely on your own. Underneath these swirling waters of struggle and flux lie deep currents of meaninglessness, isolation, and despair in a world where the modern myths of endless progress have been exhausted and the future is ambiguous.

This boy wasn't looking for a church—church wasn't even in the horizon of his awareness. He didn't know many people who went to church, and those few who did didn't talk much about it. In the California beach town where he lived, church was a minority religious option with little impact on the dominant culture. The great majority had no connection to any faith community, and non-Western religions were more popular than mainline Protestantism. People were more likely to try to find God in a walk in the woods than in an organized faith community. Those churches in town could have been the most welcoming in the world to visitors, and it wouldn't have done this boy, or most of their other neighbors, any good.

God had to come to him, *where he was*. And God did. This happened initially outside the church, through the narratives of great works of literature by Dickens and Dostoyevsky, where the Christian story plays a central role. It happened through a high school friend who modeled a life of compassion, forgiveness, and grace—a "little Christ" (to use Luther's phrase) who didn't even go to church. Through them, and through Christians who came and knocked on his college dorm door, he discovered an alternative story, one in which every human life is precious beyond measure, created for loving relationship with the source of all life. In this story, your worth is given, not earned. Rather than bearing the weight of making it all up as you go, you find yourself in a common narrative that goes back many generations. You are welcomed into a community of unlike people where difference need not be cause for division, as is so often the case in our world. You are offered forgiveness for your faults and errors, for the violence you do to others and this earth, and so are released to forgive others and break the cycle of hatred and retribution. You are claimed by a love and power beyond your own. You are held in arms of grace. And in that embrace, you are freed to participate in the restoration of human community and all creation. For this boy, this was good news indeed.

As a young man, he went on to find a home in Anglicanism, where he was nourished by a rich sacramental tradition anchored in an expansive depth of Christian teaching and practice. It was in the Episcopal Church that he discovered an expression of the Christian church where the wisdom of centuries of ordered prayer could shape his heart, mind, and imagination. In this church there was a holistic embrace of the senses, the intellect, and the body, with a passionate commitment to participating in the healing of the world. It was a community that spoke to what he—and so many other young people in today's world—yearned for deeply, a community in which to receive a new identity and new life in Christ. It was not a perfect community—indeed, sometimes it was exasperating, as any community is—yet God's grace came alive for him there.

He was eventually called to leadership in this church and began to serve a rapidly growing new start congregation in an environment not unlike where he grew up—one of America's least-churched areas. As a staff member, his primary responsibility was the formation of adults in the Christian faith, and he quickly discovered that very little could be assumed about their prior knowledge of it. On the one hand, the congregation was dramatically successful in its numerical growth (it had grown from a dozen to over a thousand members in just over a decade), yet deeper questions kept surfacing: *How do we make disciples of Jesus out of people who don't bring the Christian story with them? What does it mean to be a disciple in today's world? What does it mean to be a church member? Are they the same thing? How does the shape of life in the Episcopal Church foster depth and commitment to the way of Christ, and how does it undermine it? What does it mean to be the body of Christ in an increasingly post-Christian America? Who are we as Episcopalians and what are we here for?*

A Different Kind of Conversation

This is a book about renewing Episcopal identity for twenty-first-century America.[1] It is fitting that we begin with a story about someone outside the church, for that is where an increasing number of Americans, especially young people, find themselves today.[2] These neighbors, who come from many stories, backgrounds, and walks of life, represent the future of the Episcopal Church, if we have one.

This is a unique moment for the Episcopal Church in the U.S. For the past several decades, while the Episcopal Church has been in precipitous decline in relationship to a dramatically growing and diversifying U.S. population, the conversation has largely been focused inward, upon the church. We've tried waves of strategies and techniques to be more effective at what we've always done, to grow, to be more welcoming, or healthier. We've been convulsed by inner conflict. These strategies and struggles have not substantially altered the picture. America continues to grow and diversify, and the place of Episcopal churches in it continues to shrink in significance. The thesis of this book is that renewing Episcopal identity will not come through one more conversation about the church and how to organize it better.[3] Instead, the future of the Episcopal Church in the U.S. depends upon attending first and foremost to God's life and movement and discovering how Episcopalians are particularly gifted and called to join up with that movement. It is time to have a different kind of conversation.

It is no accident that this book begins with a story. It is my story. What is at stake in the renewal of Episcopal identity is profoundly personal for each of us, and for those whom we are called to love in Christ's name. I share my own journey as an illustration of a life liberated and transformed by coming to know God's love in Christ. For me, and for countless others outside the church like I was, the Anglican expression of Christianity offers invaluable treasures. I cannot take the story of Christ in the richness of its Anglican expression for granted. For me, and for so many of our neighbors in this changing world, these are literally matters of life and death.

Yet our common imagination in the church remains deeply shaped by a different world—the world of cultural and social establishment that marked our earlier history and roots in the Church of England. Sometimes the assumptions inherited from that world inhibit our participation in what God is doing and seeks to do in the lives of our neighbors. For instance, we still largely assume that people are looking for a church and that they will know how to find us—that we can simply welcome them when they show up (especially if they look and act like us). We assume that people come to us already Christian, and that we can just make them church members. We assume that everyone must learn our charming and antiquated customs and language, rather than claiming the vernacular principle that lies deep in our Reformation heritage of translating the church's life into the language of the people, even as language and culture change. Our approaches to mission tend to assume a place of privilege, where we dispense resources or power from the center, as benefactors. Yet at the heart of the gospel is a call to follow Christ in a posture of mutual vulnerability, where we receive God's hospitality through the neighbor or stranger. All of these themes will be explored in greater detail in the chapters that follow.

People of the Way

In the book of Acts, the early Christian movement came to be known as "the Way."[4] Jesus' followers were *people of the Way*. They were not so much members of an institution or adherents to a particular set of developed doctrines as they were disciples (learners, students, or apprentices) of a holistic way of life in Christ, through the power of the Spirit. This way of life brought them attention from the surrounding pagan society. They became both noted and notorious for their subversion of the idolatries of empire, for their compassion for society's most vulnerable, for their egalitarian community life, and for their high ethical norms.[5] Something powerfully compelling was taking place in their midst, and it pointed beyond them to God's presence and activity. For a world riven by oppression, hierarchy, authoritarianism, inequality, disease, and despair, this way of life in Christ gave tremendous hope.

> In the book of Acts, the early Christian movement came to be known as "the Way." Jesus' followers were *people of the Way*.

What might it mean for the Episcopal Church to live into a renewed identity as people of the Way of Jesus in our time and place? That is the focus of this book. Chapter 1 begins by revisiting our own unique history to explore how establishment patterns have shaped the Episcopal Church's life and ministry. Chapter 2 brings these patterns into critical conversation with today's changing U.S. setting. Chapter 3 begins with the central practice of the Eucharist to reframe and rediscover some of the key themes of Anglican theology, such as the Trinity and incarnation. The church's identity is rooted here—in God's life and love for the world. Chapter 4 reflects on baptism and invites us to imagine how to live as a reconciled community in the Spirit in a diverse America. Chapter 5 challenges us to rethink the way we typically understand hospitality so as to follow Christ into relying upon the hospitality of the stranger, rather than merely seeking to welcome the stranger into an established church. Chapter 6 beckons us to a deeper discipleship that goes beyond the ideas of church membership inherited from the era of establishment, reflecting upon the baptismal covenant and the unique gifts Anglicanism brings to twenty-first-century America. Finally, chapter 7 offers a vision for how the church's life and ministry might be reshaped for a new apostolic era.

An Identity Crisis

The Episcopal Church—and indeed, the larger Anglican community worldwide—has been facing an identity crisis for some decades now.[6] The roots go back much deeper in Anglican history, to the struggles and compromises of the English Reformation itself, as well as to the party conflicts in Anglican history between evangelicals, liberals, and Anglo-Catholics. The recent controversies in the Anglican Communion have brought the question to a boil, surfacing major cultural and theological differences in various global contexts. As a product of British colonialism, the Anglican Communion was once held together by common cultural ties to England. Yet the assumption that Anglicanism today should be equated with British or Western culture is being vigorously challenged, and rightly so, for a global fellowship of churches whose strength is now concentrated in the Southern Hemisphere.[7] Historically, Anglicans have resisted the idea that their identity lies primarily in adherence to a detailed doctrinal confession (unlike, for instance, Lutherans or Presbyterians). We have preferred instead to affirm the framework of common prayer (which of course includes a great deal of theology, expressed liturgically) and an ordered ministry. We have understood ourselves as a "creedal" rather than "confessional" tradition. We have upheld the role of bishops as signs of unity and identity with the wider Christian church, yet bishops have also become a focus of controversy. What defines Anglicanism today?

> "Who are we?" What does it mean to be an Episcopalian? We cannot be leaders within our church nor in the global community if we are unsure who we are or where God is calling us to go.

There is a movement among some in the Anglican Communion to address the identity question by moving in a confessional direction, as we see in the Jerusalem Declaration of the Global Anglican Futures Conference in 2008.[8] The emerging Anglican Covenant represents another attempt to resolve the question of identity at the level of international governance. Behind the debates and fractures in the Anglican Communion lurks the problematic legacy of Western colonialism, including the contemporary realities of globalization, which benefit Westerners disproportionately.

The focus of this book is not primarily global Anglicanism, however, but Anglican identity specifically in the United States context. In the Episcopal Church, the House of Deputies Committee on the State of the Church named the identity challenge succinctly in a 2007 report:

> "Who are we?" What does it mean to be an Episcopalian? What are our core values? How are we differentiated from other Christian faith traditions? What are our strengths and weaknesses? What are our opportunities? We cannot be leaders within our church nor in the global community if we are unsure who we are or where God is calling us to go.[9]

The Episcopal Identity Project was launched as a way to address that challenge through surveys and interviews of Episcopalians conducted from 2004–2008. The recent report issued by that project, "Around One Table: Exploring Episcopal Identity," reflects something of the ambiguity of the church today, with a diversity of themes rising to the surface.[10] This report helpfully names some of the many ways in which Episcopalians today understand their church mostly through a sociological and organizational approach. This is a fruitful way to listen to what Episcopalians think, and I will refer to its findings in the subsequent pages. Yet in the same way that responses to an opinion poll often fail to coalesce into a clear vision, the integration and coherence of these identity themes remain unresolved.

As I will explore further below, the legacy of establishment served to answer the question of identity for much of Anglicanism's history in America, from the colonial period through the mid-twentieth century. Over the past fifty years, however, there has been a dramatic cultural disestablishment of the Episcopal Church and other so-called "mainline" Protestant denominations whose roots lie in the state churches of Europe. As we will see, a variety of circumstances have made it difficult, for the most part, for Episcopalians to recognize clearly and embrace this change, which has unfolded to varying degrees in different settings around the U.S. In order to understand what new opportunities God might be opening up through this process of disestablishment, we will have to revisit some of this history, as well as attend to the dynamic new realities of American life today.

One Diocese's Journey

Several years ago, I was fortunate to participate in a renewal process within an Episcopal diocese that had been in decline and intermittent conflict for forty years.[11] Membership, baptisms, confirmations, and worship attendance had all fallen precipitously from their peaks in the mid-1960s, while the population of the area covered by the diocese had grown even more dramatically, including the addition of hundreds of thousands of immigrants from around the world. A series of attempts at strategic planning and fundraising for new mission efforts had left behind a legacy of disappointment and broken trust. Hope was at a low, and recriminations abounded. The issues were clearly deep and systemic, transcending any one bishop or group of leaders.

In order to begin to address the issues, a process was initiated aimed at large-scale participation at all levels of the church. Delegates to diocesan convention were asked questions like, "If the Episcopal Church in this area were to disappear, what would be lost?" A survey gathered the input of over 750 leaders, with nearly a thousand write-in comments. Clergy were asked to write short "This I believe" statements to articulate their own sense of theological identity. A theological position paper on mission was developed and used to spark conversations around the diocese. Teams from across the diocese visited nearly three-fourths of the congregations (all were invited to participate) to listen to where local Episcopalians sensed the Spirit at work and what forces were seen to be impeding the Spirit's movement. In all, over 2,000 grassroots members participated in the process, which was led by over 70 leaders from local churches.

As this process unfolded, several things became clear to me. First, there was a striking reluctance among these Episcopalians to talk about God. I was stunned by the secularized nature of the conversations, even when the explicit purpose of the gathering was to talk about theology! This included groups of clergy, who despite their extensive theological educations were hesitant to make assertions about God. Listening to the many layers of conversations, it was particularly rare to find a sentence in which God was the acting subject of a verb—i.e., God (or Jesus or the Spirit) actually *doing* or *saying* something. When faced with the harsh realities of a church in decline, Episcopalians in this diocese were more comfortable talking about what *they* could do to reverse the decline, like better marketing or more hospitable greeters on Sunday. With some exceptions, there was little articulated imagination for God's active presence and power in the church's midst (or in the world beyond) as a force for renewal.

Second, for a diocesan system with many lines of difference (cultural, economic, geographic, social), unity was a struggle. The Episcopal Church in this setting prided itself on its cultural diversity, which had deep historic roots. Yet how those diverse groups of Episcopalians could be united around a common sense of belonging and purpose seemed elusive. Instead, there were multiple layers of mistrust and resentment. The operative metaphors for the church, as identified by members of the diocese, were *family* and *democracy*. These metaphors warrant closer scrutiny (see chapter 4 below), but the idea that the church was a democracy of competing interests and parties where people were free to think and believe as they saw fit undercut a common sense of identity and calling.

Alongside the strong democratic ethos were monarchical expressions of leadership and authority, as reflected in Episcopal polity (church governance). The church both looked to leaders to take charge, resolve problems, and show the way, and at the same time resented their use of power when they disagreed with the direction. There was a decided ambivalence about the idea of "lordship"—the lordship of Christ and the lordship of those given authority in the church. How leadership could be exercised in a self-giving, vulnerable, empowering way—as we see in the life, death, and resurrection of Jesus—seemed to be an open question.

One of the primary mission ideals and hallmarks of identity articulated by the Episcopalians of this diocese was "inclusion." The Episcopal Church was seen as a safe space for those who felt unwelcome in churches elsewhere—especially skeptics, doubters, and lesbian, gay, bisexual, and transgender (LGBT) persons. The importance of equality for women clergy was widely affirmed. Yet there was also a reluctant acknowledgment that the membership of the Episcopal Church is skewed toward the socioeconomic elite. The ideal of inclusion, which is frequently cited more broadly as an important dimension of Episcopal identity,[12] seemed to operate selectively.

Members of this diocese identified a particular aesthetic form of worship as the greatest value to be lost if the Episcopal Church disappeared. The richness of Episcopal liturgy and music was seen as a hallmark of the church's uniqueness. Yet at the same time, the diocesan process revealed a painful sense of grief over the fact that many of the children and grandchildren of today's Episcopalians no longer participate in the church. How this particular aesthetic expression of church speaks or fails to speak to new generations and populations seemed to be a question begging to be explored.

It became clear as the renewal process came to fruition that the answers to the Episcopal Church's challenges in this particular area would not be solved by better marketing, church growth techniques, or reorganization. There were deeper issues afoot. The primary challenges were identified as *spiritual* and *theological*.[13] The Episcopal Church would need reorganization, but that must take a backseat to two major areas of focus—spiritual transformation and helping congregations reengage their changing neighborhoods.

> Episcopalians have often been too hesitant to articulate our faith. Part of our hesitancy about evangelism stems from a lack of clarity about what we stand for.

These two challenges are not unrelated. How we imagine and engage our changing neighborhoods inevitably reflects all sorts of theological assumptions. The premise of this book is that these assumptions should be carefully considered in light of Anglican theology and history and today's changed environment. Episcopalians have often been too hesitant to articulate our faith coherently and persuasively to a changing America. Part of our hesitancy about evangelism stems from a lack of clarity about what we stand for. Many Episcopalians seem more comfortable asserting what they do *not* believe than what they do believe. Now is a time to share in the work of reimagining our presence and posture as a church in relationship to God's movement to reconcile all of creation in Christ through the power of the Spirit. This book is a step in that direction, not as an exhaustive final answer, but as one attempt to wrestle creatively with rediscovering Episcopal identity within God's life and love for the world.

Another way of talking about God's love for the world is to speak of *God's mission*. Some people remain hesitant to use the term "mission" because they see it as tainted by the legacy of colonialism. For others, "mission" describes things the church does for others, often on the edges of its life. Renewed ways of understanding mission as rooted in the triune God's very life and being have emerged in the past several decades that allow us to get beyond these narrow conceptions. In the pages that follow, I will seek to describe a more expansive view of God's mission and the church's participation in it.

My hope is that this book will stimulate a different kind of conversation, a conversation that engages richly with our spiritual and theological heritage, that pays close attention to our changing world, and that invites renewed discernment for what we are called to be in light of God's healing of the world. Unless we answer the question of identity theologically and spiritually, we will simply be another secular voluntary association or nonprofit organization, a club with quaint rituals but little to offer a world in desperate need of a life-changing gospel. God's mission will pass us by, for we will fail to recognize it and our calling within it.

Excellent

The One Thing

When my wife was called as rector of the congregation where we now serve, the leadership expressed one overarching desire—"to go deeper." Founded over a century ago, this neighborhood church had a remark-

God's mission and The Church's participation in it.

able commitment to social justice ministry, both in its own city and as far away as Uganda, where it founded an orphanage for girls whose parents had died of AIDS. This was not a congregation that had closed in on itself, ignoring the world. Rather, it was busy—perhaps too busy—trying to meet the needs of the vulnerable and suffering. What was not clearly developed in all this good work was a spiritual and theological imagination for where God was active, and how this good work related to the core stories of the Christian gospel. In this sense, the call to go deeper was a call for spiritual and theological renewal.

Over the course of a few years, a particular biblical text began to take hold of the leadership's imagination—the story of Martha and Mary in Luke 10:38–42. As Martha struggles to offer hospitality to Jesus and the disciples, Mary sits at Jesus' feet, taking the traditionally male role of a disciple.

> But Martha was distracted by her many tasks; so she came to him and asked, "Lord, do you not care that my sister has left me to do all the work by myself? Tell her then to help me." But the Lord answered her, "Martha, Martha, you are worried and distracted by many things; there is need of only one thing. Mary has chosen the better part, which will not be taken away from her."

This congregation, and its members in their daily lives, could identify readily with Martha. We were used to being worried and distracted by many things—such is life in twenty-first-century America. We began to ask, *what is the "one thing" for us*? How can we attend to the presence of Jesus, both personally and corporately? What kind of focus would give us clarity amidst all the struggles, distractions, temptations, and challenges of contemporary life? How can the important work of hospitality, justice, and care for a hurting world be carried on with the spiritual attentiveness of Mary?

This congregation (like many in the Episcopal Church today, I suspect) was in need of discerning the focus that gives us new life and identity in Christ. Many congregations across America today are distracted and overwhelmed by doing too many things. Many are harried, anxious, worried, or resentful. In many places and many ways,

a spiritual + Theological renewal
martha + mary → IDENTITY

we have lost our focus, and as a result, we have become stuck—stuck in establishment patterns that struggle to engage the new world in which we find ourselves; stuck in a sense of paralysis, despair, and confusion over who we are and what we should be about; stuck in conflict, often over concerns that, while not unimportant, allow us to avoid confronting directly the massive adaptive challenges before us; stuck behind the red doors of church buildings that are too often closed to our diverse neighbors; stuck in our inability to imagine what God is up to in our midst and in the lives of people surrounding us.

For those who have walked away from active church involvement—many of them quietly—there are often very good reasons for doing so.[14] We who have stayed have in many cases not listened attentively enough to their stories and heard their concerns. Some of their discontent is a holy discontent—a rightful resistance to the ways in which we have reduced the richness of the Christian faith, distorted the image of God in the church's life, or failed to translate the gospel into language ordinary people can hear and speak. We would do well to listen to their voices, just as we must listen attentively to the stories and perspectives of neighbors who have never been part of the church in order to discern a new future.

At the same time, there are many places in the Episcopal Church where new life is breaking forth, where signs of renewal are abundant. Often, those places are on the edges, rather than in the centers of power and privilege. That proved to be the case with the diocese mentioned earlier. Today's shifting cultural environment not only brings huge challenges for mainline Protestant churches shaped by the legacy of establishment; it also brings huge opportunities for witness and engagement. Anglicanism has much to offer a postmodern society and the diverse populations of immigrants among whom America's future increasingly lies.

A Different Story

Let me end with a story about another boy. This boy grew up in a quite different home environment than the boy described at the start

who are we? what do we stand for?

of this chapter—one shaped intentionally by the story of God's love in Jesus. From before his birth, he was enveloped in the care of people not related to him by blood, but by the sisterhood and brotherhood of the body of Christ. His imagination was shaped by stories of the impossible becoming true—an oppressed and enslaved people being freed from Pharaoh's empire; a little guy named David prevailing over a giant; a father who drops everything to run and welcome a wayward son home; a savior who was crushed by people's hatred yet raised from the dead, taking us with him. This boy shares in a meal every Sunday around a table where people from many different nations and walks of life gather to receive "Jesus bread" and the experience of God's love. He is growing up in a church "village" of elders, mentors, and friends that no other community in society offers. In a world whose future seems even more uncertain than the first boy's, he shares in an ultimate promise and hope, the foretaste of which is tangible to him now.

My son, Luke, is this boy. From birth he has been nourished by participation in Episcopal churches with a rich sacramental life, deep historic roots, a generous and expansive approach to theology, and global diversity. Currently he belongs to a congregation with members from a dozen non-Western nations (a gift of the Anglican Communion and global migration). Yet the trends for Episcopal churches in the U.S. are ominous. Over the past ten years alone, the Episcopal Church has lost nearly a quarter of its average Sunday attendance. Over half of congregations have declined more than 10 percent in average Sunday attendance in the past five years. The median Sunday worship attendance for Episcopal churches in the domestic U.S. is 65 and dropping.[15] What kind of church will he and others in his generation inherit? For a church long accustomed to power and privilege, these trends are disconcerting at the least. No matter what our stories are—whether we are new to the church or come from a long tradition of membership, whether we were nurtured in familial and cultural settings shaped by Christianity

> Now is a moment to refocus our attention on the story of God's life with and for us in Christ through the power of the Spirit—to live more deeply into our identity as people of the Way.

or marked by its absence—a great deal is at stake. We are in a new day, where a different kind of conversation must guide us forward, a conversation that attends deeply to God's promises in Christ. As long as we focus on the church and try through our own best efforts to turn things around, there is no reason to believe much will change. Instead, now is a moment to refocus our attention on the story of God's life with and for us in Christ through the power of the Spirit—to live more deeply into our identity as people of the Way.

Jesus likened the reign (or kingdom) of God to a mustard seed, the tiniest of all seeds which grows into a lush, expansive tree (Mark 4:30–32). God's dreams for us are so often bigger than our own dreams for ourselves. What would it mean for us to inhabit the imagination of God's reign, where the status quo is inverted, where God comes to dwell in the womb of a pregnant teenager in a poor family in a lost corner of the empire, where what seemed least significant bears the greatest fruit? Let's explore these questions together.

Questions for
Discussion

1. Tell a story of where you met God. Was it in the church or elsewhere?

2. How did you come to the Episcopal Church? What is at stake in its renewal for you personally?

3. Do you ever feel like Martha in Luke 10, "worried and distracted by many things"? What might it mean for you personally and for your congregation communally to focus on "the one thing" that Jesus calls us to?

CHAPTER 1

THE LEGACY
of Establishment

In the San Gabriel Mountains outside of Los Angeles lies a beautiful canyon, where a scenic highway was built in the 1930s. A striking concrete arched bridge was constructed over the narrows in the canyon to join the two sides of the highway at the culmination of the project. However, a storm of unprecedented proportions arrived the winter after the bridge was completed, and a flood washed away the highway on both sides. The bridge was untouched. After a subsequent attempt to rebuild the highway higher up, the canyon walls were abandoned. Some years later, this "Bridge to Nowhere" stands aloof today, accessible only by hiking or horseback. It is used by bungee jumpers, but otherwise it remains a picturesque oddity in a changed landscape.

Many churches in the U.S. and other Western countries today resemble this bridge—beautiful structures that once connected people to God and one another, but now stand disconnected from their communities due to floods of social and cultural change.[1] Episcopalians have a particularly deep establishment legacy that shapes our churches. In order to move forward in discerning a renewed identity, we must attend closely both to where we have been and the changing world in which we find ourselves today.

The Establishment Legacy: State Church Roots

The Anglican Church began in the early Middle Ages as the church among the English people (*ecclesia Anglicana*—the church in England). It was simply that part of the Catholic Church located within the particular cultural and social setting of England. Because there is no one specific theologian or reformer that Anglicans point to as the touchstone of their identity, Anglicanism has always had a *national* character. Its identity depends in part upon the unique culture of the nation in which it finds itself. From around the year 800, the ideal of *Christendom* increasingly characterized medieval Europe, including England. Christianity became a territorial and tribal religion, supported and sanctioned by the state. Kings, queens, and other rulers were legitimized in their authority by the church, and the church was protected and encouraged by the government. This tight, symbiotic relationship between church and state prevailed for centuries, up into the modern era. During the period of Christendom, the church's mission was largely to cultivate and preserve Western culture, as well as to spread it by expanding the territory of Christendom. The era of European colonial expansion reflected the integration of church and state, as missionaries accompanied the military, political, and economic forces of colonialism in order to "Christianize" and "civilize" indigenous peoples—the two being understood interchangeably.

> Anglicanism has always had a *national* character. Its identity depends in part upon the unique culture of the nation in which it finds itself.

The English Reformation unfolded in the sixteenth century within the framework of Christendom. The Act of Supremacy, by which King Henry VIII claimed headship of the Church of England, is a powerful expression of the marriage of church and state. In this period, to be an English citizen was to be a Christian, and specifically an Anglican Christian, as more radical Protestant dissenters such as Puritans and Baptists, as well as Roman Catholics, were banned from the country (leading some, of course, to settle in America). A strong sense of national unity and identity pervaded the church and society. The Book of Common Prayer was created by Thomas Cranmer to allow the liturgy to speak in the vernacular language of the people. The church's calling was to sanctify the nation.

Establishment brought with it particular ways of organizing the church that continue to shape Anglican life, including in America. In Christendom Europe, all of the territory was divided up into parishes and dioceses, each under the authority of a monarchical rector or bishop, just as the same geography was controlled by monarchical political rulers—the king or queen, then princes, dukes, etc., down to village squires. The division of territory into dioceses and parishes reflects the reshaping of Christianity in the context of the Roman Empire (a diocese is a unit of Roman imperial governance). The church was positioned at the center, in a place of power and control.

Christianity began with different structures, however, as a movement organized along social networks in synagogues and homes in the first and second-century Mediterranean world. The early Christians used existing gathering places and relational networks to spread the gospel. When Christianity came to be officially tolerated in the Roman Empire by the Emperor Constantine in the fourth century, the church was spared the bitter persecutions which had characterized its life and witness during previous emperors. It also began to adopt more directly the cultural forms and governing structures of its host society—the Roman Empire. This should be no surprise, for at the heart of Christianity is the incarnation—God's transformational embrace of a particular culture in order to relativize and redeem all cultures. The church must take on the cultural forms of its surrounding society if it is to be the body of Christ in a given time and place. The difficult question, however, is the critical transformation of those cultural forms, for when the church uncritically absorbs (or is absorbed into) its host culture, its prophetic identity and calling are diminished. This is, in part, the dilemma facing Western Anglicans today. *Important*

Within the paradigm of Christendom, spiritual authority and care (the "cure of souls") over the people in a geographical parish or diocese was focused in the clergy. They were the "ministers" responsible for preaching the Word, celebrating the sacraments, and nurturing

→ We pay the price of playing ball.

the faith of those under their charge. This pattern of leadership represents a significant evolution from what we see in the early church, where teams of leaders (male and female) with a variety of gifts played different roles to equip the whole of the church for ministry in engagement with a non-Christian environment.[2] Once Europe was "Christianized," ministry became the province of the few and consisted primarily in taking care of an already established flock. Church membership grew by birth, no longer primarily by conversion.

The American Colonial Period

When the first English colonists arrived at Jamestown, Virginia, in 1607, they brought the Church of England with them. Anglicanism was the officially established church in the southern and some of the mid-Atlantic colonies up to the Revolution, and the state church logic of geographical parishes was transported across the Atlantic. Yet some crucial differences pertained. There were no bishops in America during the colonial period. Given the small number of ordained clergy, parishes tended to be very large. Moreover, vestries, which in England were bodies responsible primarily for helping the poor, looking after church buildings, and maintaining public roads, took on much greater power. Particularly in the southern and mid-Atlantic colonies, these vestries hired and fired clergy, for instance, planting the seeds of a more democratic form of church governance.[3]

In the eighteenth century, the predominant form of Anglicanism in the American colonies was Latitudinarianism, a rationalistic version of the faith heavily influenced by Deism. God was seen as the creator of a universe governed by natural laws that operated on their own, with little need for divine interference. Churches were spare in their decoration, with box pews, clear glass, and small communion tables. Communion was celebrated infrequently. The focus was on right living through appropriating the moral precepts taught and exemplified by Jesus. Given that the church was led by the wealthy colonial elite (who controlled the vestries), this served the purpose of encouraging good order and decorum in the colonies. There was less emphasis on God's active presence and movement in the world than on human reason and agency.

The evangelical revival or Great Awakening, a renewal movement led in part by Anglicans such as John and Charles Wesley and George Whitefield, did impact the American colonies with a call to repentance and conversion and a more emotional appeal for a personal relationship with a living God. Yet the Wesleys and Whitefield often found themselves at odds with the established church and were forced to operate outside ordinary parish life, preaching in the fields or organizing small groups in homes. They were resisted by many parish clergy, whom they criticized for spiritual lethargy.

From the Established Church to the Church of the Establishment

The American Revolution posed a major crisis for Anglicanism in the American colonies. The Church of England, with its monarchical bishops, represented the very thing that many Americans sought independence from. Clergy had sworn solemn oaths in loyalty to the king at their ordinations in England, and many left America at the outbreak of the war or openly sided with the English. When the fighting subsided, the Anglican Church was in disarray.[4]

Yet many of the most prominent leaders of the Revolution and the new United States were Anglicans. An innovative reorganization of the church was carried out in the 1780s in Philadelphia, led by the priest William White, who went on to become the first bishop of Pennsylvania. The new Protestant Episcopal Church in the United States maintained much of the DNA of its mother church, the Church of England, yet introduced a new governance structure modeled on the federalism of the U.S. government. These changes reflect the Anglican commitment that the church should embody the cultural forms of its particular national setting. The monarchical governance of the Church of England, already modified in practice by the strong role of vestries in some of the colonies, would be qualified and complemented by democratic rule, including important participation from the laity.

The Anglican Church in America went from being the officially established church to the church of the establishment as it remained favored by many of the socioeconomic elite. The resurgent Baptists and Methodists succeeded in luring away many of the lower classes through their revivalistic preaching and more open, egalitarian approaches to church leadership. As long as the Episcopal Church tended to uphold the status quo of a stratified economic system and a rationalistic faith, it failed to attract and retain wider swaths of the American populace.

> The Anglican Church in America went from being the officially established church to the church of the establishment as it remained favored by many of the socioeconomic elite.

There were nonetheless signs of significant renewal across the church amidst the difficulties of the post-Revolutionary period. For instance, William Meade led an effort to rebuild churches across Virginia in the first half of the nineteenth century. His passion for the gospel and evangelistic spirit helped a dry and disorganized church catch fire. Also in the nineteenth century, the new interest in ritual, early church theology, and sacramental piety of the Oxford Movement brought a different, richer texture to Episcopal worship in many parishes.

One particular moment in this history is worth pausing to reflect on. In the early nineteenth century, when church bodies across America were setting up voluntary mission societies for the purpose of evangelizing the burgeoning frontier and sending missionaries overseas, the Episcopal Church did the same. Yet it didn't leave this society as a structure parallel to the church. Rather, under the influence of the evangelical bishop of Ohio, Charles McIlvaine, and the high-church bishop of New Jersey, George Washington Doane, the General Convention of 1835 integrated the mission society and the church, so that every member of the Episcopal Church would be a member of the Domestic and Foreign Missionary Society.[5] Bishop McIlvaine argued that "the church is a Missionary Society, in its grand design, in the spirit and object of its Divine Founder."[6] In other words, to be sent in mission is integral to the very identity of a Christian—not something extraordinary that specialists ("missionaries") do somewhere far away, or that occupies the church from time to time (as in today's

(handwritten margin notes: "Ecumenical", "Come + see")

"mission trips," "mission budgets," or "mission projects"). Participating in God's mission of restoring all people to unity in Christ is at the heart of the church's identity. The Domestic and Foreign Missionary Society became the official legal name of the Episcopal Church in 1835 and remains so today. This is vital to recall as we renew Episcopal identity. What would it mean for us to live fully into this name, where all church members are missionaries sent into whatever neighborhood or relational network God places them in in order to share in God's work of healing all creation, according to their unique gifts?

Unfortunately, this bit of missionary DNA could not supplant the deep establishment posture that prevailed in the Episcopal Church, and the link between mission and local church membership remained largely undeveloped. As chronicled colorfully in Kit and Frederica Konolige's 1978 book, *The Power of Their Glory: America's Ruling Class: The Episcopalians*, the Episcopal Church prided itself on drawing from the nation's elite.[7] Privilege and social centrality were deep identity markers for a church with sophisticated liturgical rituals and rarified architecture concentrated in the East Coast corridors of power. Indeed, to this day, Episcopalians remain the best-educated and wealthiest Christian group in America. A 2007 Pew Forum on Religion and Public Life survey ranked Anglicans/Episcopalians behind only Hindus and Jews among religious groups in America in social status, with over half of households making an annual income over $75,000 and more than half of members being college graduates—nearly double the national average in both categories.[8]

> What would it mean for all church members to be missionaries sent into whatever neighborhood or relational network God places them in in order to share in God's work of healing all creation?

Establishment and Mission

The Episcopal Church's sense of self-confidence and social, cultural, and economic centrality led to the articulation of the "national church" ideal in the second half of the nineteenth century.[9] For an America growing in strength and power on the international stage, the Episcopal Church was seen to offer a kind of *de facto* national church through its Reformed (Protestant) faith, apostolic church order (bishops in historic succession), and democratic governance. It could combine the best of Protestant and Catholic traditions with the democracy of the nation, thereby unifying Christianity in the U.S., even without technically being the state church.

The influential New York priest William A. Muhlenberg offered a "Memorial" (proposal) to the 1853 General Convention to this effect. Muhlenberg's vision was that the Episcopal Church could reach a much larger audience and have a greater positive impact upon society through an ecumenical vision. Yet he recognized that the Episcopal Church's established habits, customs, and posture worked against its being able to reach the lower classes effectively.[10] Another prominent nineteenth-century New York priest, William Reed Huntington, saw in the Episcopal Church a unique capacity to bring together other Protestant traditions to promote Christian unity and thereby uplift the moral character of the nation.[11]

Perhaps the most visible expression of the "national church" sense of Episcopal identity and mission is the construction of Washington National Cathedral (begun in 1907, completed in 1990), representing from its perch high above the capital the Christian values that were assumed to underpin the nation. The Episcopal Church saw its role and purpose in sanctifying society from the center, with access to power and privilege. While other mainline denominations built large churches in the capital during this period, only Episcopalians would presume to call theirs *the* National Cathedral. In the words of Ian Douglas, the Episcopal Church saw itself as "a chosen people among an elect nation."[12] When the Episcopal Church began to send missionaries overseas, it followed this establishment ethos. The Episcopal Church could be part of spreading the American way of life, with its prosperity, democracy, and "civilizing" influences, particularly through education. The 1899 Annual Report of the Domestic and Foreign Missionary Society envisioned people in Africa and Asia "lifting up their hands and asking for our religion, our civilization, our schools."[13] Episcopal missionary efforts typically underplayed proselytizing or making converts in favor of attempting to build the kingdom of God on earth through social ministry and education. It is striking to note that the first country to receive Episcopal missionaries in the early nineteenth century was Greece, chosen because it was already a Christian society, though in need of greater educational and material development.[14] Throughout much of this history, the predominant establishmentarian ethos fostered approaches to mission in which confessing the faith was *implicit* rather than explicit. These linger in the Episcopal Church today.

The Establishment Legacy and Contemporary Episcopal Identity and Mission

This establishmentarian history remains alive in many ways in Episcopal approaches to mission, both in the U.S. and beyond. On the one hand, Episcopalians carry a commendable sense of responsibility for the well-being of the whole community, not just the members of the church. On the other hand, Episcopal mission has tended to operate within a *benefactor* paradigm: those with power, privilege, and resources do good works on behalf of others, yet retain their superior status. Benefactors give out of excess. This was common in the ancient world, where rulers and wealthy elites would endow public buildings or works projects as a way of contributing to the common good but also gaining glory in the public eye.[15]

Given the apparently disproportionate resources Episcopalians possess, it fits that distributing a portion of them would be integral to Episcopal mission. Charity efforts that involve giving money have a long history in the Episcopal Church as a way of addressing social issues. For instance, during the late 1960s and early 70s, the Episcopal Church sought to address racial injustice through the General Convention Special Program, whereby a portion of the denominational budget would be directed toward grassroots organizations (with controversial results).[16] The recent emphasis on the Millennium Development Goals (MDGs), in which every church and household is

> Episcopal mission has tended to operate within a *benefactor* paradigm: those with power, privilege, and resources do good works on behalf of others, yet retain their superior status.

encouraged to contribute 0.7 percent of its income to address global poverty, stands in a long tradition of such charitable efforts. The MDGs recognize the disproportionate privilege that many Episcopalians (and Americans generally) possess relative to the majority of the world's population and attempt to leverage those resources for the global good.

The MDGs function best when they open up avenues for relationships to develop across borders and cultures, for Christian mission involves something more than the mere giving of resources. It is an invitation to a deeper, more transformational engagement. We must take seriously Jesus' exchange with his disciples in Luke 22:24–27:

> A dispute also arose among them as to which one of them was to be regarded as the greatest. But he said to them, "The kings of the Gentiles lord it over them; and those in authority over them are called benefactors. But not so with you; rather the greatest among you must become like the youngest, and the leader like one who serves. For who is greater, the one who is at the table or the one who serves? Is it not the one at the table? But I am among you as one who serves."

Jesus here draws a clear distinction between the benefactors of Roman society, whose way of using their power and privilege represents a "lording over," and his own relationship with his disciples as he washes their feet. Jesus gives of his whole self, relinquishing his higher status, in order to empower his followers, to the point where at the end of his ministry with them, they move from being servants to being "friends" (John 15:15). This is a much more profound reordering of relationships than being a mere benefactor. A far more mutual, reciprocal sharing is at the heart of Jesus' community and its mission in the world.

Advocacy is also integral to Episcopal mission. As with the impulse to charity, it has generally assumed a position of social centrality with access to circles of power and decision-making. There are many significant historical instances of Episcopalians using their privilege to speak out on behalf of justice for persecuted groups. For example, during a frontier conflict between Dakota Indians and white settlers in 1862, the first Episcopal bishop of Minnesota, Henry B. Whipple, used his East Coast connections to help persuade President Lincoln to commute the death sentences of 264 Dakota prisoners (38 were still executed). During the Civil Rights era of the 1960s, many Episcopalians served on the front lines of the struggle and drew on their social prominence to try to leverage change.[17]

Seeking justice for all remains a vital dimension of Christian discipleship, as we will explore further in chapters 5 and 6. The recurring challenge for privileged Episcopalians has been to escape a tendency toward paternalism in these charity and advocacy efforts. For those with power and resources and genuine passion about justice, using one's privilege to try to assist others makes sense. As long as Episcopalians have privilege, by all means it should be leveraged for the common good. It is another thing, however, to take the deeper step of *identifying with* and *receiving from* those who are persecuted or marginalized. The first pattern tends to operate within the benefactor paradigm of establishment; the second calls us to deeper participation in Jesus' incarnational, cross-shaped mission.

The Episcopal Church has demonstrated over its history a capacity to include groups excluded by other church bodies in America. This includes African Americans, such as the group of black Methodists in Philadelphia led by Absalom Jones whose St. Thomas African Church became an Episcopal congregation in 1794. Ministry with African Americans, Native Americans, Latinos, Asians, and other ethnic minorities has been an important dimension of the Episcopal Church's identity and mission, dating back centuries. The Episcopal Church has been a pioneer in women's leadership, with women clergy since the 1970s, female presidents of the House of Deputies,

> For Episcopalians, it has often been more comfortable to give than to receive; to use our power on behalf of the vulnerable, than to be vulnerable ourselves.

and a female presiding bishop. Gays and lesbians have been welcomed openly at many levels of the church in recent years. There are many inspiring historical moments when the Episcopal Church reached out, opened doors, and made space for populations persecuted or rejected elsewhere. At the same time, minority members of the church have

Challenge - to be vulnerable

also often faced a mixed legacy of paternalism and prejudice.[18] One challenge for Episcopalians has been to live more fully into genuine, mutual relationships with one another and with diverse neighbors. For Episcopalians in the dominant culture and class, it has often been more comfortable to give than to receive; to use our power on behalf of the vulnerable, than to be vulnerable ourselves.

The commitment to diversity and inclusion within the life of the church is a prominent identity marker for contemporary Episcopalians, as noted in the introduction above. There are some rich theological impulses underpinning this commitment. Jesus' own outreach to outcasts in his society is commonly cited as an example. Another motive seems to be at work as well, however, related to the establishmentarian identity and mission of the Episcopal Church. Since the embrace of democratic polity in the late eighteenth century, Episcopalians have seen furthering democratic equality within American national life as part of their mission. This reflects the establishmentarian mission of sanctifying the nation. Episcopalians of the dominant culture have made space for other groups in part out of a sense of stewardship for democratic ideals that came with the establishment posture.

As the "national church" ideal began to disintegrate in the social upheavals of the late 1960s, the focus shifted. The Episcopal Church could no longer presume to have the capacity to sanctify the nation, nor could it expect to gather the rest of the churches under its umbrella. The Episcopal Church found itself caught flat-footed by the dramatic changes of the era, convulsed by its own inner conflict, and unable to maintain the assumption of establishment with much credibility. Episcopalians of color and women challenged the reigning paternalistic patterns of the white male leadership and demanded a deeper level of inclusion.

In the decades since, the Episcopal Church has been focused internally on a series of struggles for equality in its own life and leadership—first for racial minorities, then for the ordination of women, and most recently for the ordination of LGBT persons and the blessing of same-sex unions. These struggles represent, on the one hand,

Could no longer sanctify the nation

the working out of genuine commitments that will be explored further in this book. What also seems to be taking place is the *introversion* of the national church ideal. When the Episcopal Church found its sense of establishment identity and calling profoundly diminished in the growing pluralism and sweeping changes of late twentieth-century America, its focus turned inward, on sanctifying its own life according to democratic ideals. It could no longer presume to sanctify the nation; what was left was trying to make the church itself more democratic, in the hope that the nation would take notice. Notice how the establishment logic of the church being the central focus of society lingers here.

Much of the mission energy of the Episcopal Church in the past decades has been expended upon political goals, using political means. Whether through advocacy for more just social policy in the government or greater equality in the church's own governance, politics has often been the primary focus. The church's conversation has often taken place within secular categories, such as "rights," commonly understood in modern Enlightenment terms. While fruitful in many ways, this political emphasis also reflects continuing establishment assumptions—that the church is in a relationship of influence over the state as a moral guardian and beacon.

Episcopalians aren't alone in this—other liberal mainline Protestants have taken similar approaches, as have conservative evangelicals in the Religious Right in their attempts to "retake the nation for Christ" through political activism.[19] In the cultural wars of the late twentieth century, liberals and conservatives have been mirror images of each other in the contest for their own versions of a Christian America. Neither has succeeded, and the odds are shrinking that either will. This is because the cultural landscape has changed. The church no longer stands in a privileged position of moral authority within American society. Research among young people, for instance, has found that their negative perceptions of Christianity are shaped in part by Christian political activism.[20] When leaders of the Episcopal Church or other mainline denominations issue political statements today, who really pays attention? I am not suggesting that

Episcopalians disengage from political life. What is needed instead is a reenvisioning of the terms of that engagement. This will be discussed further in chapter 5.

Moreover, the modern emphasis on strategic, managerial solutions to the challenges facing the church also reflects establishment assumptions of control and domain. These might take the form of targeted marketing efforts, programs designed to entice spiritual consumers to participate in church, or management strategies of securing a better future through "aligning" church members around a particular vision cast by a leader. The sociologist Michel de Certeau argues that modern approaches to strategy assume the capacity to control a given environment, either through manipulation of resources, coercion, or subtler forms of influence.[21] Strategy operates from a posture of strength to remake one's surroundings according to one's own needs and desires. Its intended objects are consumers who possess many choices yet are also enmeshed, often against their will, in these larger forces.

> Churches who have embraced the consumerist paradigm often find that allegiances are fickle and commitment thin, and that it is very difficult to turn spiritual consumers into active disciples.

This is a problematic paradigm for the church to embrace. To begin with, it stands at odds with how God comes to us in Christ—not as a controlling, managerial dictator or manipulator, but as a crucified messiah who shares our place. It represents a misunderstanding of the incarnational nature of our identity as the body of Christ. Moreover, it is also increasingly ineffective, especially among younger generations weary of being manipulated by marketers everywhere they turn. Churches who have embraced the consumerist paradigm often find that allegiances are fickle and commitment thin, and that it is very difficult to turn spiritual consumers into active disciples.

So where does the Episcopal Church stand in relationship to its surrounding society in America today? Domestic Episcopal Church membership is now down below two million, out of a U.S. population of over three hundred million. In 2010, there were around 650,000 people in worship in the whole domestic Episcopal Church on an average Sunday.[22] This represents about two-tenths of a percent of the U.S. population. Episcopalians are a tiny and diminishing part of America, with much less influence than our lingering establishment self-image would suggest. Moreover, the Episcopal Church is significantly older than the U.S. population (30 percent of Episcopal members are age 65 or older, versus only 13 percent of the U.S.). It is also whiter (87 percent, versus about two-thirds of the U.S.).[23] The demographics of America are rapidly changing, and the Episcopal Church is struggling to keep up. Floods of social and cultural change are sweeping through.

Questions for Discussion

1. What establishment influences and assumptions do you see shaping your congregation's life and ministry?

2. What signs do you notice in your community of the cultural shift to a postestablishment world?

3. How does your personal story resonate with what has been discussed in this chapter? Does the loss of establishment bring a loss of something precious to you?

CHAPTER 2

A NEW
Apostolic Era

My sister Diane lives in the "none zone." Like the great majority of her friends and neighbors in Portland, Oregon, she claims no affiliation with a religious community or tradition. The Pacific Northwest has been designated the "none zone" by researchers because of the high percentage of residents who check the "none" box on religious affiliation surveys.[1] This doesn't mean that these nonaffiliated folks don't believe in God. Very few actually identify as atheists or reject religion outright. Like my sister, most claim to be spiritual people, and their lives often bear that out.

My sister and her husband (who also doesn't belong to a faith community) have sacrificially devoted themselves to nonprofit work on behalf of at-risk children, health care, and wilderness preservation. They live simply, with deep attentiveness to their environmental impact (my brother-in-law is even a vegan). Most weekends, they can be found in nature, hiking or snowshoeing. I'm sure God meets them there, as well as in their community of friends. Ethically, their lives are laudable—more so than many Christians'. They are constructing their own narratives of meaning and purpose and building their own expressions of community. The churches in their area have not meaningfully engaged them, and while they may be seeking God, they're not seeking a church.

The none zone offers a picture of some important emerging dimensions of America's future, if current trends prevail. We turn now to a closer examination of the twenty-first-century American religious and cultural setting to interpret the cultural disestablishment of Christianity, reflect further on the culture of postmodern generations, and consider the impact of immigration on the contemporary U.S. The era of establishment is rapidly giving way to a new age—what we might call a new apostolic era.

> The era of establishment is rapidly giving way to a new age—what we might call a new apostolic era.

A Shifting Religious Environment

What kind of religious landscape surrounds us in the U.S.? On the one hand, America remains an exception among Western countries for the high number of people who claim Christian adherence—about three-quarters of the population.[2] Yet in 2005, only 17.5 percent of the U.S. population was in church on an average Sunday, and only 23 percent attended church regularly (more than once a month).[3] In the U.S., so-called "mainline" Protestant churches are now functionally sidelined, claiming only a fifth of the population.[4] While the percentage of those who profess adherence to religions other than Christianity and Judaism remains small, it is growing. Perhaps most striking is the portion of the population that self-identifies with no religion—the "nones." For younger generations, this number has more than doubled in the past thirty years, now outnumbering the percentage that claims affiliation with mainline Protestantism.[5] Moreover, the depth of the Christian identity of those who claim Christian adherence in these surveys invites further scrutiny. One of the features of Christendom, or the functional establishment of the church, was that Christian beliefs and values were passed on through institutions beyond the church, such as family, schools, civic organizations, and the wider culture. That is now less and less the case. With the rapid disintegration of cultural Christianity in the United States, what kinds of beliefs, practices, and identities are functioning among those who profess to be Christian?

A Colonized Christianity?

Perhaps the most disturbing answer to this question comes from research conducted among young adults in the past decade. In *Soul Searching*, the sociologists Christian Smith and Melinda Denton describe a predominant faith that surfaced in hundreds of interviews with American teenagers from a variety of religious backgrounds, the great majority of which were Christian. They call it "Moralistic Therapeutic Deism" and define its central tenets as follows:

1. A God exists who created and orders the world and watches over human life on earth.

2. God wants people to be good, nice, and fair to each other, as taught in the Bible and by most world religions.

3. The central goal of life is to be happy and to feel good about oneself.

4. God does not need to be particularly involved in one's life except when God is needed to resolve a problem.

5. Good people go to heaven when they die.[6]

In Moralistic Therapeutic Deism, religion operates somewhere in the background of life, largely invisible. It is aimed at making one feel good about oneself and resolving personal problems. Religion is a matter of individual choice, in which real differences between faiths are assumed not to exist. God is disengaged from everyday life in the world, unless a problem arises: "God is something like a combination Divine Butler and Cosmic Therapist: he is always on call, takes care of any problems that arise, professionally helps his people to feel better about themselves, and does not become too personally involved in the process."[7] The individual is at the center of the universe. Another scholar, Alan Wolfe, draws similar conclusions, pointing out how co-opted American religion has become by American culture, including the prevalence of therapeutic individualism: "American religion survives and even flourishes not so much because it instructs

> In Moralistic Therapeutic Deism, religion operates somewhere in the background of life, largely invisible.

[handwritten margin note:] Therapy is a product of wealth & privilege —

Cannot articulate Then fa

people in the right ways to honor God but because people have ta
so many aspects of religion into their own hands."[8]

According to Smith and Denton, Moralistic Therapeutic Deism
has colonized Christianity as well as other major religious traditions
in the United States. While the young people in the study were highly
articulate about many things, they were, for the most part, remark-
ably inarticulate about matters of faith.[9] Wolfe similarly found that
"in [American] religion, whatever the Lord requires, knowledge of
his teachings is not among them. . . ."[10] Most frighteningly, Smith
points out that a young adult is more likely to become more actively
involved in church if she or he grows up in a *nonreligious* home than
in a mainline Protestant home.[11] We in the mainline denominations
are somehow inoculating our children against active Christian faith.

For many young adults, the emerging pattern is what Robert
Wuthnow calls "spiritual tinkering"—the practice of cobbling together a spirituality from whatever materials are at hand.[12] This can be
religious ideas, rituals, or practices often uprooted from their traditions of origin and floating around in the culture (such as yoga, medi-
tation, walking a labyrinth, or the principle of karma), things learned
in conversation with friends, or insights picked up from books or the
Internet. Church participation may play a role, though young people
are likely to take congregational and denominational commitments
lightly. While Christian theology affirms that divine wisdom is present in many expressions, there is little reason to believe that this approach yields the depth, coherence, and discipline that have characterized the great religious traditions, including Christianity. Rather,
spirituality is a project to work on through a series of choices made
according to one's felt needs—a fluid and shifting endeavor very different from a deep community of spiritual wisdom and accountability
into which one is apprenticed.

Life in a Secular Age

These emerging trends are shaped by a cultural current that goes
back centuries in Western culture—secularization. A shift began to
take place beginning in the sixteenth and seventeenth centuries in

You Cannot articulate what you do
not know

which the numinous, enchanted universe of
e way to a different worldview. Whereas in ear-
was understood to be charged with spiritual
nd unpredictable power of God, as well as the
sted God, like the devil—that sense of spiritual
recede in the early modern era. Instead of a world
characterized by cycles of sacred times (holy or feast days, the celebration of the mass) and "ordinary" time, everything was regularized to
the ticking of mechanical clocks. Instead of certain places (shrines,
consecrated church buildings) carrying a focused spiritual presence
(what the Celts called "thin places"), God came to be seen as distant
from daily life. What was left was a universe operating by predict-
able natural laws. Humanity's task was to discover and adhere to these
laws, and through hard work, every individual could achieve her or
his potential. The philosopher Charles Taylor describes this process
as "excarnation" (the opposite of incarnation) in which religion became disembodied from communal ritual, emotion, and practice and
focused in the mind, until humans were left alone, concentrating on
their own individual flourishing, which could be accomplished es-
sentially without God.[13]

The legacy of this secularism, despite various counterstreams,[14]
still pervades both the church and culture in Western societies today, especially the Episcopal Church. Many church members struggle
to name God's presence or activity in their daily lives or the world,
particularly in concepts, images, metaphors, or narratives from the
Christian tradition. Without the framework of cultural Christianity
to support the church, fewer and fewer church members benefit from
immersion in an integrated set of communal Christian practices, beliefs, and norms. Instead, there is a "nova effect" of moral and spiritual
options in today's society (some Christian and many not) whereby
individuals seek to find their own way, express their true selves, or
discover fulfillment.[15] For the most part, the church has not taken this
reality seriously enough, preferring instead to operate as if nothing
has changed, as if the old patterns of establishment still prevailed.

Constructing Community and Identity

One of the features of emerging late modern culture is its fluidity. Life has become radically disembedded from settled, traditional structures of meaning and belonging, especially for younger generations. To begin with, fewer and fewer people today reside within geographical communities for long periods of time, where they can benefit from the stability and nurture of generations of relationships (or find those relationships stifling!). People move frequently and switch not only jobs but whole careers multiple times over the course of their lives. Vocational identity is a product of endless choice and self-invention, constrained by the powerful disruptive forces of a globalized economy. No one's job seems secure anymore in a time of rapid economic restructuring, outsourcing, downsizing, and uncertainty.

> Life has become radically disembedded from settled, traditional structures of meaning and belonging.

Young people are waiting longer to marry, if they marry at all.[16] Divorce is increasingly common. The sociologist Anthony Giddens uses the phrase "pure relationships" to describe how people today join together solely for what they feel they can get out of a relationship. This replaces the frameworks of kinship, social duty, or traditional obligation that supported marriage, family, friendship, and community in earlier eras.[17] Pure relationships can be entered into quickly and dissolved just as easily by individuals who feel their personal needs are no longer being met.

This fosters a deep and underlying sense of insecurity as individuals find themselves unmoored from the anchors that have characterized human community and meaning in most societies. Everything is up for negotiation through individual choice, which means that one's sense of self-identity is a project of continual reflection. Very little seems given. This "liberation" from the constraints of institution, tradition, and structure brings a new kind of bondage—to self-invention, choice, and anxiety. The sociologist Zygmunt Bauman writes, "In our liquid modern times the world around us is sliced into poorly coordinated fragments while our individual lives are cut into a succession of ill-connected episodes."[18] There is a growing sense of

bondage to self invention, choice and ANXIETY

discontinuity and fragmentation in a culture increasingly shaped by technological innovation and media. Who we are and what we present to the world are now often mediated images (through Facebook, Twitter, etc.) that we endlessly revise.

This pervasive insecurity often drives people to seek community through identities cultivated *over against* one another. Bauman talks of the "voluntary ghetto" of neighborhoods dominated by private security and the fear of the stranger.[19] There is a new tribalism reflected in American culture, where people consume news from polarized media sources (Fox News, MSNBC, blogs) that confirm rather than challenge their preexisting assumptions. The multicultural movement of the late twentieth century sought to affirm diversity in American life, yet it also fostered fragmentation. Bauman says, "When mutual tolerance is coupled with indifference, communal cultures may live alongside each other, but they seldom talk to each other, and if they do they tend to use the barrel of a gun for a telephone. In a world of 'multiculturalism,' cultures may coexist but it is hard for them to benefit from a shared life."[20]

The New Immigrants

America has long been a nation of immigrants. Since the broadening of immigration policies in the 1960s, the U.S. has come to encompass a much wider array of cultures and people groups than the European-dominated earlier eras. This has unfolded not just in cities, but also in rural America. Migrant workers and immigrants constitute a major proportion of the workforce in many agricultural and food-processing industries. American suburbs are now also increasingly inhabited by immigrants. Whites are expected to be a minority in the U.S. by 2040.[21]

One of the remarkable facets of the new waves of immigrants is that they are highly likely to be Christian. This reflects the growing vitality of Christianity in the majority world. In many cases, these immigrants come to the U.S. expecting it to be a Christian country. They are surprised to find that this is not really the case. Their response is often to embrace the posture of missionaries in their adopted land, as the scholar Jehu Hanciles has documented.[22] They seek to share the gospel with Americans who may or may not have ever known it.

These immigrants typically bring culturally non-Western forms of Christianity to their American neighbors. For instance, worship in their churches often comes alive with dance, testimony, emotional expression, and embodied experiences of the Holy Spirit. This contrasts with the subdued, rationalistic expressions of Christianity many Americans are accustomed to (and many have rejected). When former colonies around the world gained independence from European powers in the twentieth century, the church flourished because the gospel was able to take root in local cultural vernaculars.[23] Now in a remarkable historical turn, Christianity is being brought back to America and Western Europe by immigrants whose parents and grandparents helped to make it more fully indigenous to Africa, Asia, and Latin America.

Life in a New Apostolic Age

These trends point toward a significantly changed religious situation in America. We have entered a new apostolic age, where the church's relationship to its surrounding environment more closely resembles the first few centuries of the church's existence in the Roman Empire than the many intervening centuries of social, cultural, and political establishment in the Christendom era. Western societies where the church was most thoroughly established (such as the countries of northern Europe, including England, where the still-legally established Church of England draws only a couple of percent of the population on a Sunday) are facing the worst crisis.

> There are striking parallels between the emerging American situation and the environment of the first few centuries after Christ in the Mediterranean world.

There are striking parallels between the emerging American situation and the environment of the first few centuries after Christ in the Mediterranean world. In those days, there was a widespread sense of uncertainty and spiritual hunger, especially for deep and ancient spiritual traditions. A global empire's technological innovation, violence, and commercial exploitation fostered the displacement and movement of people groups throughout the region. In the increasingly urbanized centers of the Roman world, there was abundant cultural and religious diversity.[24] Gaps in economic equality and cultural divisions were acute.

We live in a twenty-first-century world of globalization, economic displacement, unsustainable environmental destruction, religious conflict, terrorism, and major waves of global migration. Economic inequality is growing. Those who can afford to do so are turning away from their neighbors and surrounding communities to focus inward on an aesthetic life of pleasure-seeking and consumption.[25] America is profoundly divided. Trust has eroded. For many people, there is a sense that the modern Western myths of technological progress and mastery have run their course. A new spiritual hunger has emerged as people seek meaning, purpose, community, and sustainable ways of living on this earth together amidst global diversity.

The Promise of Disestablishment

There are profound new opportunities for Episcopalians in today's changed American setting. Many people in today's world are looking for an authentic *lived faith*, not just a set of propositions to believe in, rules to live by, or an institution to belong to. They are eager to tap into ancient wisdom that helps them make sense out of life in today's world. They are aware of the diversity in American life and wonder how various differences can be reconciled rather than divide us. They are seeking a word of healing, hope, liberation, and promise—a trustworthy word in which they can abide and find life. They want to contribute toward building a trustworthy world.

A generation or two ago, the assumption was that in order to be culturally credible, the church had to downplay God. Cultural relevance required "demythologizing" the faith, rendering everything in secular terms.[26] Times have changed. The myths of secularization have proven to be just that—a particular Western cultural wave that has already crested and is being replaced by a resurgent interest in spirituality, even as the overarching cosmology of secularism continues to shape ordinary life in the West. It should be noted that in today's world context, it is nonsecularized and non-Westernized Christianity that is exploding with growth. We in Western cultures have much to learn about the gospel from our sisters and brothers in the world church, and vice versa.

Anglicanism offers a richly textured Christianity with ancient roots, expansive sources, a living commitment to justice and reconciliation, and space for people to explore, question, and grow along the way. It embodies the wisdom of centuries, not just the latest fads. Its historical embrace of whatever cultural context it finds itself in mandates that it speak the language of the people. At the same time, it is inhibited in many places by traditionalism that obscures the power of its traditions; by elitism that restricts its treasures; and by a lack of theological and spiritual clarity and urgency that would fuel a renewed sense of purpose. Episcopalians still largely assume that people will find the church, rather than recognizing that disestablishment pushes us out into the world, on the arms of God, to serve and embrace the stranger wherever she or he is.

Accepting disestablishment brings with it a whole new posture for the church. As with the church of the original apostolic era, we can rediscover our identity as a *sent people* (the root of "apostle" is "sent"). We need no longer concentrate our energy on preserving and maintaining the structures inherited from a different era if they inhibit our ability to connect with people where they are in today's world. We can be freed to reshape the life and language of the church's worship and witness, retaining the richness and wisdom that we have inherited while translating and innovating anew.

> As with the church of the original apostolic era, we can rediscover our identity as a *sent people*.

This is a far more exciting, risky, adventurous, and transformational path than simply doing what we've always done. Rather than inhabiting the modern narrative of linear progress, we can live more deeply into the core story of our tradition—death and resurrection. This means that we will likely have to let go of some treasured aspects of the church's life in order for fresh expressions of the gospel to be born. We will have to make space for those on the edges of the church's life to innovate the future and join them in it. We will have to adopt new and ancient habits and practices as we seek to discern what God is up to in our midst and what kind of future God is bringing forth. We will have to learn to be sowers and midwives of the church of tomorrow—cultivators of new life from which God will give the growth. This means reengaging the core stories of our faith in order to rediscover how we might be called to participate in God's restoration of the world in Christ, through the power of the Spirit. That is the focus of the next chapter.

Questions for Discussion

1. Think about people you know who don't participate in church or any faith community. Why do you think they don't? What can the church learn from them?

2. What might those people be missing? How might you communicate that to them or provide them a taste of it?

3. How might the church offer a different sense of belonging, meaning, purpose, and security than the dominant culture in America?

CHAPTER 3

A PEOPLE...

Sharing Communion

Melissa had left the church long ago, in her early twenties. Frustrated and angry at the dualism she experienced in the conservative Baptist faith of her childhood and youth, she had spent years exploring pagan and Buddhist spiritualities. After her daughter was born, Melissa struggled with two years of depression, during which time she also suffered a few miscarriages. At an utter loss, she sensed a leading one day to seek a Protestant church where communion was offered every week. She simply wanted to pray and receive the comfort of the Eucharist.

Melissa found an Episcopal church advertising a healing Eucharist and showed up. She remembers thinking, *I am defective. I don't know how to mother my child or do anything successfully. Please heal me. I haven't prayed much for the last twenty years, but please help me anyway.* The lectionary readings that day happened to be all about bread: manna from heaven feeding the starving Israelites, Jesus as the bread of heaven. What she heard whispered in the liturgy was this: *You aren't defective. You're hungry. Eat.*

Over the next few weeks, as she returned, the readings were still all about bread. Her self-condemnation and hopelessness began to give way to a different understanding: she was hungry. Hungry for peace, community, and adult company. Hungry to feel a sense of spiritual connection and belonging. Hungry for self-confidence as a mother. Hungry for anything that was nourishing. A few years later, Melissa is now a confirmed Episcopalian who leads the healing prayer team at her church, helping others to experience God's healing and grace.

Communion and Community

Every Sunday at ordinary Episcopal churches, something extraordinary takes place. In a society in which tables of hospitality are mostly closed off to strangers, a public feast is held. You don't need to buy a ticket to this meal. Not everyone necessarily knows each other; not everyone gets along perfectly, but they come together nonetheless. The food is simple stuff—bread and wine—about to become something more than itself. As the story is told and songs are sung, a change takes place. Hearts are lifted. The brokenness in the lives of each of the participants, and the brokenness of the world, is brought into focus. Healing begins to pour through it. Lives turned inward are opened outward. In the midst of the messiness and richness of this meal is the presence of Jesus, felt and known through the Spirit, tasted in the bread and wine, inviting us and the whole of the world into community with God.

> Episcopalians gather around the table, finding there an expression of God's grace and love, an experience of what it means to be the church in the Spirit's power.

The Episcopal Church, like other Christian churches, exists first and foremost because of God's life and love for the world. Renewing Episcopal identity after the era of establishment calls us to reflect on the nature of that life and love, for it is there that we rediscover who we are on the deepest level. Over the past several decades, the Eucharist has become the central practice shaping Episcopal churches. It is the primary form of weekly worship in the great majority of Episcopal congregations in America. No matter whether liberal or conservative, or high, low, or broad church, Episcopalians gather around the table, finding there an expression of God's grace and love, an experience of what it means to be the church in the Spirit's power, and healing and hope for service in the world.

When the church gathers around the bread and wine, retells the story of God's relationship with the world, remembers Jesus' last meal with his disciples, and experiences a foretaste of the heavenly banquet, it shares a thanksgiving meal ("Eucharist" literally means "thanksgiving"). We gather in God's presence to give thanks for the gift of life, to offer symbols of daily life (the bread and wine) to be transformed into symbols of the new creation, and to recall how God has bound us together in the Spirit. In a society of many false promises and insecure futures, we affirm God's promised future—the restoration of all that God has made. At the center of that celebration is the reality of suffering and death, which God takes up and absorbs into God's own life in the cross of Jesus. This is a meal that calls forth the depths of who we are and what we experience in this broken world, rather than glossing over them. We bring to it our humanity in its imperfection, and we are renewed there.

In the Book of Common Prayer, the second half of the Eucharistic liturgy is called the "Holy Communion." The word "communion" (Greek *koinonia*) is one of the richest terms in the New Testament. It means sharing, participation, fellowship, belonging, togetherness, solidarity, unity, reciprocity, and mutuality. Communion is the reconciliation of difference into a common life. It means the opening up of self to others in a shared sense of identity. It brings together things that were once estranged. Communion describes not only what takes place in the celebration of the Lord's Supper, but also the heart of God's own life and love for the world in the Trinity, in whose image we were created. It is fitting that we begin our rediscovery of Episcopal identity there.

God's Ecstatic Communal Life

When American Christians hear the word "God," I suspect few think of a divine community. We might imagine an immaterial force; a transcendent, fatherly (or motherly) creator; or a personal Jesus with whom we are in relationship. These all reflect important dimensions of the Christian view of God. Yet they are incomplete. Without understanding the wider relationality of God's life as Trinity, we miss out. Not only do we lose the richness of the biblical witness and the

Trinity

wisdom of centuries of theological reflection by faithful Christians, but we also misunderstand what it means for humanity to be created in God's image. In the process, we miss what it means for the church to share that image in a hurting world.

The Bible speaks about God in multifaceted ways—from the Spirit who moved over the waters at the beginning of creation (Genesis 1); to the gardener God who forms humanity out of clay (Genesis 2); to the mysterious presence in the burning bush whose name (Hebrew YHWH) means "I am who I am" or "I will be what I will be" (Exodus 3); to the mother who cries out in labor pains for her people (Isaiah 42); to the Spirit who anoints Jesus to announce the arrival of God's jubilee and liberation (Luke 4); to the crucified Lord, who subverts Caesar's lordship and reigns with mercy and justice (Revelation 21). At several places, God is referred to as a unity of Father, Son, and Holy Spirit.[1] As Christians in the first few centuries sought to make sense out of the relationship between the Jesus they had known as Lord, the Spirit they experienced in community, and the God of Israel to whom the scriptures gave witness, they developed the doctrine of the Trinity. The Trinity is a way of talking about the richness of God's communal life. From a Christian perspective, God is a relational community of three persons: Father (or Mother or Creator),[2] Son, and Spirit. The identities of these three persons are defined by their relationships with one another. Without the Father, the Son would not be a son, and vice versa. The Spirit unites and opens their life to the world. There is difference and otherness at the heart of God's own life without division or confusion. All three act together in God's relationship with the world in history, yet each also has a distinct personhood and role.

> As Christians in the first few centuries sought to make sense out of the relationship between the Jesus they had known as Lord, the Spirit they experienced in community, and the God of Israel in scriptures, they developed the doctrine of the Trinity.

The eighth-century theologian John of Damascus used a term to describe the relational life of the Trinity that bears attention today. The term is *perichoresis* in Greek, and it literally means "circulating around the neighborhood" (other meanings are whirl, rotation, mutual indwelling, or interpenetration).[3] In some ancient cities (as in some cities in the world today), it was common for the populace to gather in the evening in a public square and its surrounding streets to stroll, mingle, and greet one another. This fluid movement of people was an expression of community life in which families and strangers made space for one another, and everyone participated in a larger sense of belonging. In the Christian theological tradition, *perichoresis* came to describe the dynamic, open, shared character of God's communal life.

The Trinity is not a community closed in on itself up in heaven, sealed off from the world, but rather a community whose own identity is found in freely sharing life and love with others. Another ancient way of saying this is that God's communal life is *ecstatic*—outward reaching, generative, and creative (from the Greek word *ekstasis*, literally standing outside oneself).[4] It is in God's nature to create others to share in God's life. Humanity was created for belonging with God, one another, and the whole fabric of creation. We are made for interdependence. In Genesis 1 we read of how God created humanity in God's own image and entrusted us with a unique vocation to care collaboratively and creatively for the world. There is space in this relationship to choose, to develop, to grow. Just as God cares for the world, so are we to care for it in creativity and freedom.

Excellent

The Breaking and Restoration of Community

Yet the Genesis story speaks to the deep human tendency to misuse that freedom, to choose self-interest over other-interest, to seek *in*dependence rather than *inter*dependence, to refuse to trust God. Because of this, the Creator's intent for a life of communion—reconciled difference, in a dynamic and creative community—is thwarted and fractured. Human relationships with God, one another, and the earth break down. Miscommunication and mistrust enter the picture, and the human vocation becomes messy, painful, and ambiguous. This biblical narrative describes in mythical and theological terms the matrix of human estrangement into which we are all born, and from which we cannot free ourselves.

Humanity created for Belonging — God, one another + the world.

God's response is not to forsake humanity, but rather to restore community, beginning with a family, Abraham and Sarah. God calls Abraham and Sarah to go on a journey of faith, promising to bless them *so that they will be a blessing* to the world (Genesis 12). Being called or chosen in the Bible is not a privilege, but a responsibility.[5] Despite Abraham and Sarah's mistakes and mistrust along the way, God grows their family into a clan, a clan that becomes a people who eventually find themselves enslaved in Egypt. Through Moses, Aaron, and Miriam, God challenges the imperial power and culture of control of Pharaoh.[6] He liberates the slaves, leading them into the wilderness, a place of uncertainty, testing, and spiritual formation.

In the wilderness, Israel learns to become a community in right relationship (covenant) with God. For those accustomed to the dependencies of slavery, it is not an easy process. God gives the law through Moses to shape their life in distinction from their neighbors, calling them to paths of justice and mercy. After long years of wandering, in which a generation passes, they settle in the land promised by God. As they do so, they are told to recall their own painful history and make provision for the stranger, the alien, the widow, and the orphan (Exodus 22–23, Leviticus 19). Their identity is to be found in relationship to the holy God who called and freed them, so that they might show forth God's vision for just and merciful human community to all the nations.

Yet when Israel gains its own imperial strength and wealth, it begins to lose this identity. The Spirit of God raises up prophets to call the people back to faithfulness. When their intransigence prevails, they are violently displaced into exile, where they must learn anew what it means to be God's people. Living as exiles among foreign cultures and foreign gods, Israel is charged to seek the welfare and peace of the places to which they have been sent, to develop relationships, to plant gardens, and to embody a faithful witness there (Jeremiah 29).

Sharing Our Place

Empires come and go, and eventually Israel returns to the land under the oversight of other powers than its own. By the time the Romans succeed the Persians and Greeks, the calling to be a light to the nations seems difficult to sustain, at best. Into this situation of imperial oppression and economic privation the story takes a definitive turn. In Jesus, God chooses to participate fully in human life in order to restore humanity to participation in God's communal life. Jesus is born into a family from an obscure village on the edge of empire, under rather suspicious circumstances to a young mother. He is raised in the family of a skilled laborer, having been a refugee with his parents in Egypt. These beginnings are less than auspicious, needless to say, but that's how God works—choosing to show up in the unlikeliest of places, through the unlikeliest people, to bless the world. The very strangeness of the story is integral to its power.

Jesus is the one in whom God's vision for human life is restored. He lives in profound interdependence with God, gathering a community of friends and followers who are apprenticed into his way. In the power of the Spirit, Jesus reclaims and reinterprets God's promises to Israel, expanding them to include all nations. He challenges the authorities (whether religious or political) who would box God into a narrow set of regulations and rules. He heals the sick and delivers the possessed. He confronts those who would oppress by teaching about God's reign, which calls into question every human power and authority.

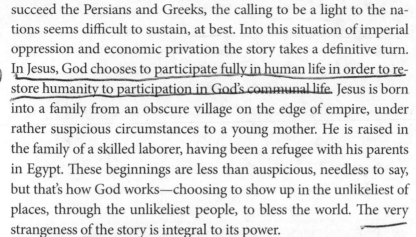

In Jesus, God chooses to participate fully in human life in order to restore humanity to participation in God's communal life.

Jesus' teaching about and embodiment of the reign of God, consistent with the message of the prophets, introduces a powerful message of reconciliation into a world divided by hostility, violence, religious conflict, and ethnic tensions. He reaches out and embraces those excluded from the community of the promise, redrawing the lines of the blessed and the cursed. Samaritans, women, Gentiles, tax collectors, prostitutes, the notorious, and the resented are all recipients of Jesus' mercy and invitation to new life. The reconciliation of difference through loving the neighbor—even and especially when the neighbor is an outsider—is at the heart of the ministry of Jesus.

God's reign is a provocative and mysterious reality, showing up in surprising places. As an expression of God's agency and power, it can be neither built nor controlled by us. Rather, Jesus invites us to seek, enter, receive, or inherit it. It is holistic, touching on every aspect of life. The reign is profoundly personal and also communal, social, and political. It is not to be confused with this world's governments, for Jesus refused to become the political revolutionary or worldly king many wanted him to be. This reign is present now, but also yet to be fulfilled.

In the incarnation, God chooses to work through the particular for the sake of the universal, to inhabit fully one culture and historical moment in the person of Jesus so as to break down the claim that any one culture or historical moment is divinely privileged. All cultures may bear God's presence and promise, and all may distort that presence and promise. Jesus reveals anew what God's creation design for humanity is—a life of communion with God and others, a life of care, collaboration, and loving service. The incarnation is God's ultimate act of identification with us on our terms, in our humanity, in our cultures and historical situations. In Jesus, God shares our place. In this loving commitment to us, in the midst of our very brokenness, God offers us grace—the grace of unconditional love, forgiveness for our faults, and healed relationships.

Dying Outside the Gates

Jesus's loving embrace of those who are estranged from God extends all the way to the cross, where he is condemned and tortured. The cross stands at the heart of God's story as a provocative and perverse symbol. If first-century visitors entered Episcopal churches today, they would likely be stunned to see our aesthetically ornate crosses; in the ancient world the cross was a despised symbol. What Jesus suffered in the crucifixion was the worst thing that could happen to someone in his day. Crucifixion was cursed under the Jewish law.[7] For Rome, it was the means of publicly dealing with rebellious slaves and traitors to the empire. In an honor/shame society, it was the most degrading and humiliating thing that could happen to you, carried out in vulnerability, nakedness, and excruciating pain. Jesus died outside the gates of

Jerusalem because that is where such shameful and unclean acts were relegated to take place.

Yet by dying on a cross, Jesus shares the place of the shunned, excluded, and condemned. Through his godforsaken death, Jesus demonstrates that no human place or situation is, in fact, godforsaken.[8] God has gone with us into the deepest valleys of the human condition, into death itself. What happens in the passion and death of Jesus is a reversal of what humans have so often assumed about God—that God is aloof, detached, uncontaminated by the world, and that we're on our own in this mess we've created. In the incarnation and passion, God is present in the most painful and surprising places.

> Jesus looses us from bonds of estrangement we cannot break on our own and breaks down unjust structures and ways of ordering human life so that all are empowered and freed.

Notice what Jesus did *not* do when faced with unjust persecution, mob violence, and humiliating torture. He did not return that violence, enacting retribution. Instead, Jesus opened his arms in vulnerable embrace and absorbed that violence in order to break its cycle: "Father, forgive them, for they do not know what they are doing" (Luke 23:34). In order to deal with human violence, God took it into his own life, suffering it within his own person. The cross was not just something that happened to Jesus in isolation; it was also a trauma for God the Father and God the Spirit.[9] Some say that to lose a child is the worst thing that can happen to you; God knows this personally.

In many Episcopal churches today, the cross gets far less attention than Jesus' ministry with social outcasts. Yet they cannot be separated. Jesus' ministry of incarnational participation in the lives of those to whom he was sent was not just a matter of enlightened social teaching. It went much deeper, into his utter identification with them in their suffering and alienation. The cross is not so much the means of satisfying a righteous Father's sense of justice as it is God's definitive intervention in the patterns of human violence and injustice to break them. God becomes both a victim and a liberator. Jesus is our redeemer because he looses us from bonds of estrangement we cannot break on our own, restores our place in God's community, and breaks down unjust structures and ways of ordering human life so that all are empowered and freed. God's justice is a restorative justice bought at the greatest personal cost.

The cross is not the end of the story, of course. God raised Jesus from the dead as a tangible sign of victory over the powers of evil and a pledge that death is not the end of human community. Rather, our promised future in Christ is a future of communion—reconciled community with God through Jesus in the power of the Spirit, and with all those who participate in this promise from every time and place. The resurrection is God's making things new. Salvation in biblical terms is much larger than individual souls getting into heaven. Rather, it is nothing less than the restoration of all of creation—a new heaven and new earth (2 Corinthians 5, Revelation 21). The resurrection of Jesus is a kind of first fruits or down payment on God's promised future for the world—the heavenly banquet around which people from every tribe and nation share in God's communal hospitality and feast together (Revelation 7).

Continuing Jesus's Ministry

It is in this story of God's restoring love for the world, God's mission, that the church finds its identity. Jesus leaves as his legacy a *community* that embodies God's promises and reconciliation to the world, in the power of the Spirit. The birth of the church at Pentecost (Acts 2) represents the continuation and expansion of Jesus's ministry through his followers to all nations. As the Spirit fills the room, people from many places hear the gospel in their native languages. The good news of God in Jesus is translated from the very outset of the church into different cultural forms. It is universal precisely through its embrace of cultural diversity.[10]

> Jesus leaves as his legacy a *community* that embodies God's promises and reconciliation to the world.

As the book of Acts unfolds, the Spirit of God leads the early Christian community across lines of difference into the world. Against their tendency to hunker down in Jerusalem out of fear, the Spirit breaks

Salvation is the Restoration of all Creation.

open their communal life for others to share in it, driving them across cultural boundaries. Peter is challenged in a dream to share in table fellowship with the Gentile Cornelius and to baptize his household (Acts 10). Paul, Barnabas, and others go forth to Antioch and other Gentile cities, where they give witness in the language and terms of Greco-Roman culture. Along the way, resistance, suffering, and persecution mark their path. Throughout, the Spirit draws, challenges, empowers, and teaches them.[11]

The church is a product of and participant in God's mission or love for the world. It exists to embody, in the tangible form of its communal life and through its relational witness, the good news announced by Jesus. God's presence and love are by no means restricted to the church, yet the church holds the interpretive key to them as the body of Christ.[12] It is a *human* community—as evident in the New Testament itself, where the disciples struggle to understand Jesus and the early church is full of conflict. Nonetheless, it is a *holy* community—sanctified by the presence of the Spirit of God, sharing the Lord's baptism and meal, and bearing the cross.[13] God works through ordinary people—typically those the world would disqualify—to do extraordinary things. That is the nature of the Christian story.

Within this community, the Spirit gives different gifts, which together shape the church's ministry to the world. Paul's letters describe these gifts as integral to the communion, or shared belonging, that constitutes Christian life.

> For as in one body we have many members, and not all the members have the same function, so we, who are many, are one body in Christ, and individually we are members one of another. We have gifts that differ according to the grace given to us: prophecy, in proportion to faith; ministry, in ministering; the teacher, in teaching; the exhorter, in exhortation; the giver, in generosity; the leader, in diligence; the compassionate, in cheerfulness. (Romans 12:4–8)

All the members of the body are necessary for its functioning, and all gifts contribute vitally to the church's life and witness. Ministry is not something done by the few to or for the many, but rather something done by everyone, in different forms, for everyone else, especially those outside the church's community. This mutuality reflects the participatory nature of God's engagement with the world in Christ.

Authority and leadership in the New Testament churches conform to this sense of mutuality, as the disciples go forth in pairs or teams, and those at the center (Jerusalem) learn new insights about the gospel from the edges (Antioch). Against those who would claim their superior apostolic credentials, Paul boasts only in his suffering and weakness (2 Corinthians). He patiently and passionately urges the churches that he founded to a life of faithfulness, yet he uses persuasion, not coercion.

This pattern of self-giving leadership echoes the cross-shaped nature of God's authority in Christ. Perhaps no other passage articulates this more powerfully than Philippians 2:5–11:

> Let the same mind be in you that was in Christ Jesus,
> who, though he was in the form of God,
>> did not regard equality with God as something to be exploited,
> but emptied himself,
>> taking the form of a slave,
>> being born in human likeness.
> And being found in human form,
>> he humbled himself
>> and became obedient to the point of death—
>> even death on a cross.
> Therefore God also highly exalted him
>> and gave him the name
>> that is above every name,
> so that at the name of Jesus
>> every knee should bend,
>> in heaven and on earth and under the earth,
>> and every tongue should confess that Jesus Christ is Lord,
> to the glory of God the Father.

What does it mean for every knee to bend to a Lord who gives up power to take the form of a slave, becoming dependent upon humanity? In a church rightly concerned about patriarchy and the misuse of power, we sometimes forget how radically Jesus redefines fatherhood and authority. The one whom Jesus called "Father" is the one whose identity lies in a Trinitarian community of equality, who gives of his life to empower others, who patiently bears with humanity in its rejections of his love, who suffers the death of his own son so that we might be liberated.

Likewise, the early Christians did something profoundly subversive when they used the term "lord" (Greek *kyrios*) for Jesus. It was a term that was typically applied to Caesar—the archetype of imperial overlords. To say that someone crucified by the empire, who refused political or economic power and washed his disciples' feet like a slave, was *Lord* was nothing short of revolutionary. It's easy to lose the dramatic sense of irony here—and the challenge that it lays down to our own human pretensions to power in the church and world. Within God's Trinitarian life, power is shared mutually and expansively, given and received, rather than hoarded and abused.

Promise and Participation

The church is a community of *promise* and *participation*. It is a community of promise because it receives and bears God's grace and forgiveness in Christ. It offers an alternative ending to the world's stories. Against those who would suggest that life is merely the battle of the strongest against the weakest, or an inexorable trajectory of increasing material prosperity, or a cynical and meaningless exercise in self-invention, the church points toward the new creation in the resurrection of Jesus as the ultimate ending for the human story. It is a community of promise because it trusts in God's abiding presence and power in the very midst of the fallen powers and structures of this world.

It is a community of participation because it shares in God's communal life through the Spirit and the sacraments.[14] Its identity is found in participating in God's life and love for the world, not just in caring for its own members, but loving its neighbors the same way God loved us in Christ. We find our identity by going where Christ went. <u>Mission isn't just something</u> that Christ delegates to the church <u>to do on his behalf.</u> Rather, <u>God remains the primary actor in mis-</u><u>sion, and we join up with what God is doing.</u> That means entering the reality, culture, language, and concerns of our neighbors in a posture of humility. It means becoming learners, expecting to receive as much as we give. It means speaking a word of healing and hope only in the midst of deep listening. It means accompanying our neighbors patiently and passionately, in the presence of the Lord who washed his disciples' feet, the God who turns strangers into friends.

To accompany is, literally, to break bread with. <u>This is one of the</u> <u>most common ways Jesus shared life with people in his day—eating at</u> <u>table together.</u> In every gospel story of Jesus sharing a meal, even when he takes the role of host, he relies upon the hospitality provided by others. For instance, the feeding of the five thousand depends upon the young boy's provision of fish and bread. One of the most powerful table stories is the journey to Emmaus in Luke 24. Jesus draws alongside two disheartened and confused disciples struggling to make sense out of what had just taken place in Jerusalem. Jesus interprets these events for them in light of God's long story with God's people, going back to Moses and the prophets. Then he shares a meal with them, at their insistence. And they come to recognize him in the breaking of bread. <u>What does it mean for us to walk</u> <u>with people in our world, helping them make sense out of their lives</u> <u>and struggles, and to share in their hospitality,</u> where God's presence comes alive between us?

> The Eucharist has taken on centrality in Episcopal life because it is the way we interpret God's gift of communion, God's gracious hospitality, and God's presence in the brokenness of our world.

Living Eucharistically → *Central*

The Eucharist has taken on centrality in Episcopal life because it is the way we interpret God's gift of communion, God's gracious hospitality, and God's presence in the brokenness of our world. When we gather around the Eucharistic table, we may gain a different perspective on every other table in our lives—our own dinner tables, the tables with

metaphor of the church as a round table

which we share food and fellowship with friends, relatives, and strangers, the tables at which important decisions are made that affect the common good. The breaking of the bread is a tangible symbol of the brokenness and violence of human life, focused in the cross of Christ. That brokenness is not an end, not an ultimate defeat. Through God's entering into and overcoming it, we receive healing. The powers of self-centeredness and domination are themselves broken in the brokenness of the cross. We are fed by and share in the costly reconciliation that is at the heart of the Christian life, becoming a people living no longer for ourselves. As we eat the body and drink the blood of Christ in the bread and wine, we discover new identities, with all our creaturely and cultural distinctiveness, as the body of Christ. Just as that body is given freely, so are we given to nourish the world.

> The God of Jesus Christ is a God on the move, a God circulating around the neighborhood, a God already alive and present in the homes and lives of our neighbors.

As a way of discovering its own communal identity, an Episcopal congregation in the Midwest used the storytelling process of Appreciative Inquiry[15] to identify its spiritual gifts. Through hours of conversations in small groups in which people shared stories of when the congregation was at its best, one theme rose above all others— food. This congregation loves to share meals together. It feeds the homeless regularly. It provides food for members and neighbors who are sick or struggling. The Eucharist is celebrated every week. As the congregational team that led the storytelling process reflected on these comments, they began to connect the threads. God's hospitality in the Eucharist has everything to do with the tables set for community sharing and conversation after church, as well as the provision for the needy. Recognizing this, the congregation began to ask, *who is hungry in our neighborhood? How does God's gift of communion open us up to share community and hospitality with others in our world?*

The Eucharist brings into focus God's life with and for us. The great sixteenth-century Anglican theologian Richard Hooker wrote eloquently of our mutual participation in Christ, which finds its most profound expression in the sacraments.[16] In Christ we have a new identity in God with one another. We become partakers in the divine nature (2 Peter 1:4).[17] We are joined through the Spirit with God in Christ. There is a new belonging that we know concretely through baptism and the Eucharist—a belonging to God and others. Through them, God embraces us, acts in us, and sends us into the world.

The God of Jesus Christ is a God on the move, a God circulating around the neighborhood, a God already alive and present in the homes and lives of our neighbors. Through the Spirit, God continues to create and recreate, renewing the face of the earth. Through Christ God comes to us as the stranger, the guest, bearing the wounds of human vulnerability. The world's future belongs to this God of community, who seeks tirelessly to restore and draw all things into right relationship. The church has an integral role to play in that restoration. We turn next to exploring more deeply the shape of its communal life and witness.

Questions for Discussion

1. What does the Eucharist mean to you?

2. When have you experienced the creation or restoration of community? How do you imagine God might have been at work there?

3. What signs do you notice of God circulating around your neighborhood? How might God be present? What might God be up to?

CHAPTER 4

A PEOPLE . . .

Reconciled in Difference

The two children being baptized that Sunday morning began their journeys far away—one the son of new Americans from Zimbabwe and Zambia, the other a daughter descended from nineteenth-century European immigrants. Their family stories intersected in an Episcopal church in St. Paul, at the baptismal font, where they were joined by God's grace to a unique community—the household of God. In the waters of baptism, Kunashe and Sylvie became brother and sister, joining countless other sisters and brothers in a household unlike any other, stretching across space and time, across nations and cultures. Through baptism, these two were symbolically drowned and raised again, receiving God's forgiveness and being knit into a community of reconciliation, as the assembly of sisters and brothers prayed and pledged to support them in their life in Christ.

Reconciling Communities

Christian mission is about the creation and restoration of community in the image of God. Just as the Eucharist is a profound expression of this reality, so too is baptism. In baptism, God acts in and through us to claim us as God's own, to bind us through Christ and the Spirit to God and one another. We receive a new identity in baptism, moving from being isolated individuals to being *persons* who share in an interdependent life of communion.[1] In this sense our personhood comes to reflect the personhood of the triune God, a relational personhood defined with and for others. God's own being in the Trinity assumes otherness—the distinction of Father, Son, and Spirit is integral to the unity and relationality of God. So often in our world and in the church, we assume that unity depends upon sameness, that differences must be removed in order for people to come together. Baptism into the name of the Trinity says otherwise. We are joined by God into this unique household, sharing in God's communal life, with all our creaturely and cultural distinctiveness. In this community, such differences need not divide us; rather, they are part of our reconciliation in Christ through the Spirit and our identity as a community of promise.

> We receive a new identity in baptism, moving from being isolated individuals to being *persons* who share in an interdependent life of communion.

The triune God engages the world in reconciliation—bringing those who had been estranged into right relationship, without erasing created differences. Throughout the New Testament, a variety of texts speak to God's creation of a new community in Christ that breaks down the cultural, ethnic, and religious divisions that divide the world. Ephesians says of Christ: "For he is our peace; in his flesh he has made both groups into one and has broken down the dividing wall, that is, the hostility between us. . . . So then you are no longer strangers and aliens, but you are citizens with the saints and also members of the household of God" (Ephesians 2:14, 19). As Paul makes clear in Galatians, being joined to Christ does not mean having to renounce one's own culture to adopt another; the new Gentile Christians do not have to become culturally Jewish in order to be Christian. As the African missiologist Lamin Sanneh observes, Christianity is remarkable for the way it is constantly translated into different cultures.[2] Unlike most major world religions, the language spoken by its founder (Aramaic) is not the dominant language of the faith today. Already within the New Testament itself, the good news has been translated into different languages and cultural forms. This process is part of the dynamic, incarnational character of Christianity.

[handwritten margin note] reconciliation - bringing the estranged into right relationship without erasing created difference

In the baptismal liturgy in the Prayer Book, we say together to the newly baptized, "We receive you into the household of God."[3] This draws on New Testament language for the church. Households in the ancient world were more expansive than what contemporary Americans think of when they use the term "family." They included slaves, apprentices, tutors, and extended relatives. Episcopalians and other mainline Protestants commonly refer to their churches as "families." In the modern American context, however, it is easy for this metaphor to be understood in an insular way. Just as many modern American families are intimate and tightly knit, usually with no room for the stranger, our churches can also close in on themselves. Families are, after all, the most difficult human system to join—you have to be born, married, or adopted into them.[4] It is better to use the term "household" than "family" when describing the church's communal identity. In the household of God, no one can claim privilege of place; we are all adopted children via our baptism. It is *God's* household—not the household of one culture, tribe, or ethnicity. We don't own or control it. In order to be fully God's household in a particular place, the church ought to reflect the diversity present there; this is integral to the church's mission of giving witness to Christ's reconciliation of the world. Sound difficult to achieve? Many Episcopal churches struggle, for all sorts of good reasons, to realize such a vision of diversity in their congregational life. In order to understand the church's identity as a reconciled and reconciling community, we must explore more deeply some of our current ways of understanding difference in the church.

The Ideal of Inclusion

"Inclusion" as a central purpose for the Episcopal Church came to prominence in the later decades of the twentieth century. It was perhaps most famously articulated by Presiding Bishop Edmond Browning in his vision of a church in which "there will be no outcasts."[5] In the era of multiculturalism, this recognized the many varieties of difference in American life and the need to make space for all to participate. Inclusion is a noble ideal that acknowledges the reality that the church has been exclusive, discriminatory, and inhospitable to various populations for much of its life. Such behavior is at odds with the church's God-given identity as a community of reconciliation in Christ. As described in chapter 3, Jesus crossed many social boundaries in his ministry as he intentionally reached out and extended grace to those excluded by society.

As a primary way of conceiving of difference in the church's life, "inclusion" has significant limitations. It tends to assume that the primary movement is *attractional*—drawing people into the church's existing life who would otherwise be left out. The logic of establishment lingers here in the sense that others are to join what we already have. This assumes a church culture and community life already established, into which others are incorporated, rather than a movement outward to create new community with those neighbors on the terms of *their* cultures. As anyone who has moved to a different congregation knows, it is difficult, in existing communities with long-established habits, practices, and norms, for the established culture to be renegotiated by newcomers. It can take many years—sometimes decades—to gain trust and authority within an existing church. I know of congregations where "new people" have been members for twenty years!

It is thus easy for the rhetoric around "inclusion" to mask something else—the retention of power and centrality within the life of the church by those long accustomed to it while inviting others to participate around the edges. Inclusion falls short of a more radical decentering or change of identity in relation to the neighbor. Within the rubric of "inclusion," we can make ourselves feel good about how welcoming we are without actually changing our churches that much or risking entering our neighbor's world.

I recall a visit our family made to an Episcopal church in another city several years ago. The church's website prominently promised "radical hospitality," as did a big banner hung out in front of the large gothic sanctuary, which looked like a castle. When we walked in, however, no one greeted us. With our young son (around three at the time, though a practiced churchgoer), we took up seats. As the beautiful, formal liturgy commenced, we noticed there were no other children in the sanctuary. My son only needed to rustle his drawing paper for our neighbors to turn and cast a glance that let us know such distractions were not welcome. I looked back and realized that the narthex was partitioned off by a glass screen; this is where I was expected to keep him during the service. I dutifully took him back there, while the people at the "welcome" table in the narthex ignored us. If our family—a white Episcopal clergy couple with a relatively quiet child—felt unwelcome at this church, how would the overwhelming majority of unchurched neighbors surrounding them in this city feel if they came? How would neighbors of color or different socioeconomic status experience this church, which was almost exclusively white, well-heeled, and older in age? "Radical hospitality" is a wonderful ideal, and I don't doubt the sincerity of the leaders who proclaimed it at this church. Living into the reality is another thing, however, especially when it is conceived in terms of including people into what we already have.

In practice, the Episcopal Church has been best at including those who share its existing predominant socioeconomic class and culture. Inclusion in the Episcopal Church has been directed selectively, mostly toward women, racial minorities, and LGBT persons—all of whom continue to face various forms of exclusion in the church and society. The opening up of leadership roles and participation for these populations is no small thing—the Episcopal Church has led the way in breaking down major walls. Yet it is striking, for all the talk about inclusion, how much less emphasis there has been on broadening the church's appeal to people of different education or income levels, for instance. Sociologically, many Roman Catholic and Pentecostal congregations—both of which are quite "exclusive" in terms of their patriarchal leadership policies and conservative social teaching—are actually much more successful at realizing socioeconomic diversity in their membership. The sociologists Robert Putnam and David Campbell found that bridging of social classes is much more likely to occur among evangelical Protestants than mainline Protestants in America.[6]

> It is striking, for all the talk about inclusion, how much less emphasis there has been on broadening the church's appeal to people of different education or income levels.

I once attended a clergy gathering at which a bishop spoke about the importance of an inclusive church, and then said, "The only ones who should be excluded are those who would exclude." On the one hand, this bishop was naming an important reality—that reconciled communities of love require those who persist in hatefulness to change, or else they do violence to the community. On the other hand, his statement was more complicated than it might seem. I looked around the room and saw a handful of clergy from predominantly immigrant churches. They were among the few people of color in the room. The bishop was referring to homosexuality in his message about inclusion, and many immigrant congregations adhere to traditional teachings on sexual ethics. Were these immigrant leaders and churches then to be excluded in the name of inclusion? Who decides? The bishop, standing in the center of the room and holding power? "Inclusion" can be a dicey thing. While the impulse toward it is a genuine and generous one, we must find more adequate ways of thinking about difference in the church's life.

Democracy and Diversity

Alongside the ideal of inclusion, democracy is a key identity marker for Episcopalians. Many are proud that the church reflects the Enlightenment values of the United States Constitution and Bill of Rights, with their stress on individual rights, self-determination, limited powers, open participation, and equality. The Episcopal Church's adoption of a modified form of democratic governance was a truly innovative development in the history of Anglicanism. Sometimes Anglicans from other nations in the world fail to understand how unique it is, especially in its provisions for elected lay governance. Compared with many alternatives, the democratic governance of the Episcopal Church has a lot going for it.

 Democracy operates in multiple and at times conflicting ways in the life of the church, however, and it is worth probing a bit more deeply. We might begin by distinguishing three historic forms of democracy—aristocratic, modern liberal, and deliberative.[7] *Aristocratic*

aristocrate

(1)

democracy (also known as republican democracy) is rooted in the tradition and thought of Aristotle. It involves an elite leadership acknowledged by the citizenry to be virtuous and then granted authority to rule, often with little public accountability. This is because aristocratic democracy assumes a shared set of communal values in society. Aristocratic leaders are assumed to embody and adhere to those values and virtues. This form of democracy operates within Episcopal Church polity in the power of elected vestries, rectors, and bishops for life. Compared to churches with congregational polity, where the whole congregation votes on key matters, Episcopalians entrust key leaders to make these decisions for them. Bishops are granted tenure until mandatory retirement, unlike some denominations in which they must be reelected.

A second form of democracy is *modern liberal democracy,* which emerged in the Enlightenment. As defined in its classic form by John Locke, in this form of democracy, private citizens enter freely and contractually into social relationships to pursue their private economic and lifestyle choices. The public sphere is not assumed to consist of shared communal values, but rather competing private interests. Political power is achieved through electing like-minded representatives who will act in those interests. In this case, the majority tends to win, and minorities have little recourse except trying to influence the process as best they can. Modern liberal democracy functions in Episcopal polity through the diocesan and General Convention assemblies, at which legislation is enacted through a sometimes contentious political process.

Modern liberal democracy also deeply shapes the ethos of the church today, as many Episcopalians have embraced the modern Western cultural assumption that faith is merely a private matter. In the Episcopal Church in particular, there is a strong sense that what you believe is a matter of individual choice, not necessarily of communal consensus. (This is ironic, of course, for a church whose identity is focused on the practice of "common prayer.") Through this view, the Episcopal Church has made space for a lot of people whose doubts and unorthodox interpretations of Christianity would place *who are we? what do we believe in?*

> John Locke's vision
> of church as a society
> of people who freely
> associate to get their
> spiritual needs met has
> become the dominant
> mode in America. It has
> a deep downside.

them outside the boundaries of historic creeds, confessions, and many church traditions. Modern liberal democracy offers autonomy and freedom, which can be liberating. The challenge is discovering unity, consensus, shared discernment, and ways of "bearing with one another in love" (Ephesians 4:2) amidst difference. There is a real danger of our distinctive Christian identity being diluted, which accounts in part for the church's current identity crisis.

John Locke's vision of church as a society of people who freely associate to get their spiritual needs met has become the dominant mode in America.[8] It has a deep downside. When people aren't feeling spiritually satisfied, they simply reaffiliate somewhere else, or nowhere at all. Combined with a culture of consumerism, this has fostered a highly individualistic understanding of church organized around personal satisfaction.[9] There is little imagination for being a community shaped by deeper bonds, belonging, and discipleship in Christ.

In England and colonial America, the parish system historically provided a container for diversity and unity. Everyone within a certain geographical area would go to their parish church, mixing the rich, the poor, and everyone in between. This was contingent upon the church being established in a Christian society, however. In the U.S. after the American Revolution, the parish system began to fragment pretty quickly. Under the influence of modern liberal democracy, the Episcopal Church has become a boutique, niche church serving a narrow audience of self-selecting members.[10] In the diocesan renewal process described earlier, one Episcopalian described the Episcopal Church as being "like the audience for National Public Radio—small, but discerning." This candid comment may describe accurately the well-educated, liberal constituency of many Episcopal congregations. Yet this kind of posture can too easily lead us to abdicate responsibility for engaging neighbors who differ from us. We assume that those who want to worship how we already worship or who think like we do will find us and we can then "include" them.[11]

Quakers / Unitarians

Finally, there is *deliberative democracy*, which seeks to cultivate public, communal norms and values through practices of communication, reasoning, argument, and action.[12] Like liberal democracy, it emphasizes widespread participation and seeks equality. In this case, leaders are responsible for developing spaces of shared dialogue about the common good. The tables of conversation must be set carefully to attend to power dynamics in the community. In a society in which diversity and competition have led to increasing fragmentation and mistrust, deliberative democracy offers a promising corrective. Rather than the church being focused on private spiritual needs, it can be a community of conversation and practice for the common good.[13] This means gathering around the important questions and challenges of the day and interpreting them together in light of the biblical story, the Christian theological tradition, and the best thinking from various fields of human inquiry. This approach reflects the classic Anglican method of engaging scripture, tradition, and reason, as outlined by Richard Hooker centuries ago. The church then becomes a space of meaning-making and learning through communal conversation, not simply a refuge for private spiritual yearnings. Decisions that shape the personal and communal life and witness of the community are informed by deeper engagement with one another and with the riches of our theological heritage.

> Rather than the church being focused on private spiritual needs, it can be a community of conversation and practice for the common good.

This discussion of inclusion and democracy demonstrates some of the complexities of living into the ideal of diversity that many Episcopalians profess. The church's dominant ways of understanding diversity—inclusion and democracy, alongside the rather contradictory idea of church as "family"—provide little grounds for the kind of deeper communal reconciliation described in the New Testament. Inclusion, democracy, and family are secular categories. In themselves, they offer little imagination for God's presence and agency in the life of the church and in relationship to the neighbor. The patterns of establishment and the reality of human sinfulness complicate the church's ability to live into a diverse vision through its own best efforts. Biblically, reconciled communities are the work of the Spirit of God in and among us. It's time to reflect more deeply on a theological vision for how God creates and sustains communities of difference.

The Public Spirit

When Episcopalians talk about the Holy Spirit, I suspect many tend to imagine him/her[14] as an "it"—an abstract force at work generally in the universe, or perhaps a feeling alive within believers' hearts. It is less common to conceive of the Spirit as a *personal public presence* who makes God's power knowable.[15] One of the great casualties of the modern secular worldview described in chapter 2 is a loss of imagination for God's active presence in the world. This has everything to do with a loss of attention to the Holy Spirit.

Biblically, the Spirit of God is integral to the creation and restoration of community. That community affirms difference without fracturing into individualism. Created differences are cultivated while unjust, debilitating differences are reordered and removed.[16] For instance, the prophet Joel writes (in a passage echoed in Acts 2):

> I will pour out my spirit on all flesh;
>> your sons and your daughters shall prophesy,
> your old men shall dream dreams,
>> and your young men shall see visions.
> Even on the male and female slaves,
>> in those days, I will pour out my spirit. (2:28–29)

The Spirit is not restricted to elites, the privileged, or people in formal authority, but moves through and empowers even those who are socially disempowered. The Spirit does not erase difference, but rather reconciles it into right relationship.

> The Spirit does not erase difference, but rather reconciles it into right relationship.

The Bible's testimony to the Spirit's work is rich and extensive, ranging from the beginning of Genesis, where the Spirit moves over the face of the waters at creation, to the heavenly visions of Revelation. It's worth drawing out some key threads along the way. In the period of the Judges and the early monarchy, the Spirit works powerfully in uniting and delivering the community of Israel from threats facing it, often by raising up leaders from the grass roots.[17] When Israel establishes the power and security of its own empire, the Spirit raises up prophets to call the people to justice and mercy. Often, these prophets are ordinary people with no outward qualifications for their role. Yet God chooses to speak through them to rebuke and warn the powerful, and to cast visions of just community for all. Those prophets typically speak from positions of vulnerability, not privilege. Isaiah's discussion of the suffering servant, the promised bearer of righteousness, is a powerful example of this.[18] Jesus's own ministry is Spirit-led, as announced vividly in his reading from Isaiah 61 in his hometown synagogue:

> "The Spirit of the Lord is upon me,
>   because he has anointed me to bring good news to the poor.
> He has sent me to proclaim release to the captives
>   and recovery of sight to the blind,
> to let the oppressed go free,
>   to proclaim the year of the Lord's favor."
> And he rolled up the scroll, gave it back to the attendant, and sat down. The eyes of all in the synagogue were fixed on him. Then he began to say to them, "Today this scripture has been fulfilled in your hearing." (Luke 4:18–21)

Jesus is the concrete bearer of the Spirit who acts to liberate people, restore justice, and offer mercy to those estranged. The Spirit creates a "force field" of love that reconciles people into new forms of community. Differences that had previously been the cause of enmity now become the basis of a rich diversity.[19]

This is expressed in the birth of the Christian community in Acts 2 and worked out in Paul's discussions of spiritual gifts in the body of Christ (Romans 12, 1 Corinthians 12, Ephesians 4). Diverse gifts are given by the Spirit for the common good. The presence of diversity is necessary for the body to function and fulfill its calling. Throughout the book of Acts, the Spirit animates the growth and expansion of the

Christian community as cultural lines are crossed and the gospel is translated into different expressions. The Spirit is poured out in surprising and provocative ways as the new community of Christ becomes a visible sign of God's promised future of reconciling all people and all things.

This *public, community-forming, and restoring* dimension of the Spirit's work is vital for the Episcopal Church to recover in order to live into its ideals for diversity and reconciliation. Biblically, reconciliation is *God's* work in which we participate. It is not our project or program, or primarily a human effort. Our role is that of ambassadors (2 Corinthians 5:20)—those caught up through the Spirit in God's reconciliation of the world in Christ who are charged with the sacred commission of announcing and interpreting that reconciliation across cultural and social lines.

> Our role is that of ambassadors—those who are charged with the sacred commission of announcing and interpreting God's reconciliation across cultural and social lines.

Think for a moment about this metaphor of ambassador. In order to represent the authorities that send them faithfully, ambassadors must stay well connected. At the same time, they must be fluent in the language and culture of the place to which they are sent and in which they are guests. They must be able to speak in terms that will be understood. They have the freedom to interpret the message creatively, but always with accountability. This biblical image of being ambassadors of reconciliation is a rich way to imagine our calling as the church.

The church can give credible witness to the new humanity reconciled and restored in Christ without being an idealized community of perfect diversity and harmony. The New Testament community had an abundant share of misunderstandings, failures, and conflicts! Sin mars our ability to imitate the perfect Trinitarian community of reconciled difference. We live in the between-times, and we will always fall short. Yet that doesn't disqualify us from the Spirit doing powerful work in and through us. Recall that it is the impetuous Peter, who betrayed Christ three times, who is named "the rock" upon which Christ builds his church. Peter represents all of us—sometimes clear, sometimes clueless, able to grasp what God is doing only partially, but enough to participate meaningfully. Christ has restored God's image in humanity perfectly to free us from the burden of trying (and failing) to do so.[20] We can share, through the reconciling power of the Spirit, in his life and witness.

But we can't do it alone. We do it through participating in what God has already done, is doing, and wants to do in us and in the lives of our neighbors. This requires prayerful attentiveness to the Spirit's presence and movement—classically known as *discernment*, which we will explore further. This means cultivating our ability to imagine together what God is doing in our midst and in the world around us.

Following the Neighbor's Lead

The Spirit does surprising things. St. Peter's in Ripon, Wisconsin, was founded 150 years ago and is about the median size for an Episcopal congregation, with sixty on an average Sunday. It had no grand dreams for becoming a diverse, multicultural congregation. Yet one day several years ago, a local English as a Second Language (ESL) class needed to find a new place to meet. The church offered itself. Having met there for a while, the students (native Spanish-speakers) asked to tour the sanctuary. They inquired whether masses were ever held in Spanish. The answer was *not yet*.

The rector, who speaks Spanish, decided to give it a try. Twenty-five showed up for the first Spanish liturgy. It is now a weekly offering, with anywhere between half a dozen and thirty attendees. Two members of the vestry (including the new junior warden) now come from that service. Major feasts like the Easter Vigil and Maundy Thursday are bilingual. A trip to Costa Rica, where the church has a companion relationship, deepened connections between the English and Spanish speakers as they mutually relied upon the hospitality of others. A ninety-nine-year old Anglo member decided to start worshipping at the Spanish service, and several Anglo members are beginning to learn Spanish.

This transformation happened because St. Peter's was open to being led by the Spirit and by some of the new Americans in their town.

By opening the door to a community need (the ESL class), they ended up opening their doors to a new community and to the transformation of their own. Rather than try to incorporate these new neighbors into their existing worship and culture, they followed the neighbors' initiative to shape a worship experience that fit the neighbors' culture and language. The congregation is now working intentionally to deepen the bridging of cultures and relationships as a tangible sign of their reconciliation in Christ. This was helped in part by the Anglo members having been reminded that their ancestors were once immigrants too. The whole experience has been an organic process of trial and experimentation.

The Spirit creates and restores community by decentering and reshaping our individual identities in a communal direction. Instead of the modern Enlightenment myth of the autonomous individual, free to do whatever he or she pleases, we recognize that our lives are embedded in a fabric of interdependence. Our very personhood is shaped by others, not primarily over against them. For those accustomed to power and privilege in society, this means opening up and sharing that power, as Christ did with us. For those deprived of power and authority, as Christ was on the cross, it means receiving power and rising in new patterns of relationship. This community which we enter in baptism is not one of coercive homogeneity. Rather, it depends upon difference and otherness to thrive.

This kind of transformation of identity and community doesn't come easily. If we're on our own to do it through our own willpower, I find little reason for hope that we will accomplish it. But when we wait expectantly upon and recognize the Spirit's action, the picture changes. The public work of the Holy Spirit changes our hearts and minds, knits us together, reorders human community for justice and mercy, and invites us to participate in a new future. Baptism defines this new community in Christ, as we are claimed by God and marked by the Holy Spirit as Christ's own forever.

In Acts 2, a gathering of people at Pentecost from many nations speaking many languages finds itself transformed into a new community. The Spirit bridges cultures and breaks down walls. The community shares life and resources abundantly. This reconciled community doesn't remain in the Jerusalem Temple for long, however. Soon, the Spirit pushes it out to form new community with people in the regions beyond. This happens in part because of persecution and resistance from established authorities. It is also an expression of the basic nature of the body of Christ—to be a community through whom God is reconciling the world. This movement outward is the focus of the next chapter.

Questions for
Discussion

1. How have relationships with those different from you influenced your identity and way of seeing the world?

2. Have you ever been an outsider to a community? What did it take (or would it take) for you to be welcomed without having to give up your uniqueness?

3. When have you experienced God's Spirit alive and moving within your congregation's life? What about in the neighborhood or in your daily life? Share a story of this.

CHAPTER 5

A PEOPLE . . .

Seeking the World's Hospitality

St. James Episcopal Church in Great Barrington is the oldest congregation in the Diocese of Western Massachusetts, founded in 1762 by missionaries from the Society for the Propagation of the Gospel. Its first full-time rector, Gideon Bostwick, was a missionary priest who baptized over two thousand people in Massachusetts, Vermont, New York, and environs. By the late 1850s, St. James had become a quintessential establishment church—located in its third building, a traditional gothic stone structure on a prominent corner in town. Its peak days of membership and social prominence had long faded by the start of the twenty-first century, however, and the congregation struggled to maintain its building and reach out to the surrounding community.

On July 31, 2008, a large part of the stone wall behind the altar crumbled and fell onto the rector's car parked outside. Thankfully, no one was hurt. But the building was quickly declared unsafe by the authorities, and the church eventually learned it faced a bill of about $5 million to address widespread structural problems and needed renovations. St. James became homeless. The first Sunday "after the fall of the wall," the congregation met in the conference room of the local hospital. Unable to retrieve many of the church supplies left in the building, they had to ask an important question: *what is essential to being church together?*

The people of St. James found that much of what they had taken for granted for so many years could, in fact, be left behind. After a time of searching for a Sunday meeting space, they settled on the banquet hall of a brewpub—or as they call it, "the bar." Midweek worship is conducted in the boardroom of an insurance company, and the vestry meets in a hospital conference room. In its long years of functional establishment, this church had carried out its stately, dignified worship, expecting anyone interested to find them on their terms. Now they had to ask others for shelter. They had to express their public worship and witness in spaces owned by others and claimed by the community at large.

One of the things they realized quickly is that the church is, in fact, *the people*, not the building (theirs has since been sold). Their experience of the Eucharist has been heightened as they come to see that "secular" public space can, in fact, be sacred. Moreover, another nearby congregation, St. George's, Lee, MA, had recently made a proactive choice to sell its building and let its rector find another call in the face of dwindling membership trends. The people of St. George's decided to join St. James for worship at the bar. There is a new spirit of openness—not only to other Episcopalians (with whom they previously might have seen themselves competing) but also to the stranger, to other neighbors in the community. If you're new to church, a bar or banquet hall is a lot less intimidating a place to show up at than an imposing stone church building. Disestablishment—in this case, sudden and disruptive—has opened doors, sending these Episcopalians into the arms of the community and opening up their life along the way.

Following an Itinerant Messiah

In many churches today, the primary question being asked is, *how do we get more members?* Behind this is often a painful awareness of the patterns of institutional decline and the need for more "bodies and bucks" in the pews to sustain things. This is not the primary question we should be asking. Instead, we should be wondering, *what is God up to in our neighborhood?*[1] How do we join up with it? What is our unique calling, both personally and communally? How are we gifted to contribute? This is a very different kind of question to answer, for it forces us to attend prayerfully and carefully to God's life and movement in the biblical narrative, the wisdom of faithful Christians through the ages, in our own midst, and in the lives of our neighbors. Instead of strategizing about how to attract or include those neighbors into our churches, we are pushed out, into the world, to rely upon their hospitality. That is how Christ comes to us.

> We should be wondering, *What is God up to in our neighborhood?* How do we join up with it? What is our unique calling, both personally and communally? How are we gifted to contribute?

One of the things that the paradigm of establishment did to the church was to try to fix the sacred geographically—within consecrated church buildings, tended by consecrated people (clergy). While Christian theology has historically affirmed God's presence and movement beyond the assembled community in the wider world, establishment tended to deemphasize it. If you wanted to meet God, you "went to church"—meaning to a building set aside for this purpose. If you wanted to introduce people to God, you invited them "to church." Outside the "church" was secular space, seen as ambiguous, threatening, or at the least indifferent to the sacred.

When we gather around Word and Sacrament, we receive vital, life-giving, tangible expressions of God's presence that allow us to interpret the divine outside of the assembled community, as I have argued above. Yet this narrowed imagination about God's presence, which corresponds with the rise of Christendom during the Middle Ages, bears some responsibility for so many people leaving the church today. They reject a God domesticated to rather arcane rituals done by designated "holy" people set apart from them and confined in antiquated buildings. They seek ways of experiencing God in daily life, in nature, in ordinary relationships. Despite its best intentions, the church has often failed to offer these people practices and language that would help them recognize the sacred faithfully in their world. The church has also communicated the message (explicitly and implicitly) that God primarily shows up on Sunday mornings or in church meetings and not at the job site, during the daily commute, at the office, or around the dinner table at home. Establishment's legacy of a church-centric imagination hinders us from seeing God at work in the neighborhood, which is unfortunate, because that's where our future lies.

In the incarnation, God entrusts Godself to the hospitality of the world. The Word "who was with God and who was God" came into the world, "yet the world did not know him. He came to what was his own, and his own people did not accept him" (John 1:1, 10–11). Due to the machinations of an imperial census, Jesus was born on the road, in a stable. He was forced with his family to flee into Egypt as a refugee from government persecution. When he began his public ministry, his own hometown, Nazareth, rejected him for proclaiming that God's grace extended even to Israel's enemies (Luke 4:14–30).

This messiah spent his ministry as an itinerant, going where the people were in various villages and towns. He didn't stay in one place and expect them to come to him. He depended upon their provision for his daily meals, for a roof over his head. Sometimes, this was provided by members of his inner circle, such as the sisters Martha and Mary of Bethany. Other times, he rather scandalously invited himself to dinner parties with "sinners," such as the notoriously corrupt tax collector Zacchaeus. He ate at the homes of the prominent and religiously pure, such as Pharisees, as well as among the great crowds of the poor. He violated multiple social taboos by asking the Samaritan woman at the well to give him a drink of water (John 4). Even the Last Supper was held in a rented room. In his resurrection appearances, he asks for food from the disciples. God, the great host of the universe, comes among us as a guest.

Receiving Hospitality

Hospitality functions in the Christian tradition in multiple ways.[2] For Episcopalians, the logic of establishment has prioritized the church seeking to *offer* hospitality to our neighbors, inviting them to our feasts. That is a worthy thing to do, and we should do it as sensitively and graciously as possible. God comes to us as a needy stranger whom we are called to feed, clothe, and embrace, as Jesus makes clear in Matthew 25:42–45. Yet this is only half of the picture. As followers of Jesus, we must also learn to *be* guests, to rely upon the hospitality of the neighborhood.

This comes into focus in the story of Jesus sending the seventy disciples in Luke 10:1–12.[3] Jesus appoints the seventy to go ahead of him into towns and villages where they may meet resistance: "I am sending you out like lambs into the midst of wolves" (10:3). Then he tells them to depend upon the hospitality of the villagers for their well-being: "Carry no purse, no bag, no sandals; and greet no one on the road. Whatever house you enter, first say, 'Peace to this house!'" (10:4–5). Jesus tells them not to move about from house to house and to eat what is set before them.

Consider for a moment how intimate the living quarters of first-century Palestinian houses were. These were one- or two-room dwellings housing multiple generations and often animals. The disciples are to dwell on the cultural terms of these neighbors, in close proximity and over enough time that real relationships can form. They heal the sick and proclaim that God's reign is present in the very midst of this encounter. It is only when a village refuses to accept the peace that the judgment is pronounced—and it is a harsh one. Such a rejection is a refusal of God's reign of mercy, justice, and reconciliation.

Hospitality here is reversed—the disciples do not offer hospitality *to* the neighbor or stranger, but seek the hospitality *of* the neighbor or stranger, with all the vulnerability that implies. Going "without purse, bag, or sandals" is almost unimaginable to Episcopalians, given how dependent we have been on giving away money in our mission efforts. The sociologist Mark Chaves found that social service mission efforts in American churches tend to be programmatic and periodic, without opportunities to form significant relationships:

> Congregation-based social service involvement is more typically composed of small groups of volunteers who are enlisted to carry out well-defined periodic tasks, usually focused on a very specific need. They do not, in general, require more than fleeting personal contact with needy people, entail a particularly holistic approach to individuals' crosscutting needs, or aim at character transformation. . . . These

programs do not, in general, bring the poor into community with the people of the serving congregation.[4]

This means that we miss a central opportunity—to receive *from* those whom we serve. Without the building of community, especially across lines of social difference, it's hard for there to be mutuality and reciprocity, for us to grow and be transformed as the Spirit works between us and our neighbor. The invitation to Christian mission becomes thinned to a transaction that leaves us largely untouched.

The fact that Jesus' disciples cannot take any baggage or money that would secure their well-being independent of the neighbors to whom they are sent means that they must depend upon those neighbors. They must come with open hands, ready to receive—or they will starve and have nowhere to sleep. They cannot be finicky about the food offered to them. They must adopt a posture of real humility. The giving here goes both ways, as does the receiving. There is genuine mutuality and reciprocity. As described in chapter 3 above, God's Trinitarian community is one of dynamic mutuality and reciprocity. The creation of communities of reciprocity in God's image is integral to Christian mission and the church's identity.

> Without the building of community, especially across lines of social difference, it's hard for there to be mutuality and reciprocity, for us to grow and be transformed as the Spirit works between us and our neighbor.

Some are suggesting that Luke 10:1–12 replace the Great Commission (Matthew 28:19–20) as the key mission text for the church in Western cultures today.[5] Matthew's charge to "make disciples of all nations" became a seminal text that inspired the modern mission movement from the late eighteenth through the twentieth centuries. Within the frameworks of establishment and colonialism, it took on a life of its own. Western Christians saw their mandate as the conversion of the world to faith in Christ, and they had the cultural, economic, military, and political power to try to accomplish it. This problematic legacy has left an allergic reaction to the term "mission" in many churches today, as guilt lingers over the many abuses of power that accompanied modern colonial missions.

Imagine what might have happened had that text from Matthew been read in a more thoroughly Trinitarian way, where "baptizing them in the name of the Father, Son, and Holy Spirit" was understood as inviting people into a community of reconciled difference with a crucified messiah at its heart? What if "disciples" had been understood as "learners," not as mere subjects or objects of conversion? Moreover, what if Luke 10:1–12 had instead been the guiding text, and missionaries went without resources and with open hands to depend upon those to whom they were sent as they shared the peace? The mingling of political, economic, and military power with the church that characterized the era of establishment skewed the church's reading of many texts. Now is a time to repent of the abuses of colonialism, in which the Episcopal Church and other Western church bodies were actively complicit, and engage our neighbors differently.

We must do so without losing our confidence for a public faith, however. Sometimes, it can seem like Episcopalians are "ashamed of the gospel" (Romans 1:16) due to their worry about perpetuating the coercive posture of colonial mission. Faith becomes relegated to private individual preference, rather than a public truth claim and invitation for developing community with the neighbor. Churches that embrace this approach will die when their members die—they have nothing to share. We are called to a bold confidence in Christ, but its basis must shift dramatically from that of the establishment mode. Rather than trusting in our political, economic, or cultural power to secure our best ideas about the neighbor's future, we are invited to join up with God's ongoing movement in the neighborhood, trusting that the Spirit is at work in the life of our neighbors, that we meet God there, and that by going with empty hands as learners we will experience God's peace. We must go as Christ came to us—as guests, in a posture of humility and dependence.

Taking the Plunge

If you think the Episcopal Church's establishment legacy is problematic, consider what the Dutch Reformed Church in South Africa faces as it tries to renew its identity after the apartheid era. The Dutch Reformed Church was the church that theologically sanctioned apart-

Plunging ~ Kirby

heid. It came to symbolize the oppressiveness of the white, Afrikaans-speaking regime of that period. When South Africa entered a new period of reconciliation and transformation in the 1990s, the Dutch Reformed Church faced a major challenge—to reflect the new South Africa by embracing the diverse neighbors they had cut themselves off from for so many years. These neighbors were not likely to attend their churches, even with their best efforts at a warm welcome. The picture is further complicated by the fact that South Africa has eleven official languages.

> Rather than invite the neighbors to come to some event or program at church, the primary agenda is cultivating community, listening to people's stories and dreams, and beginning to share life together.

Christians in the Dutch Reformed Church and other predominantly white churches in South Africa have had to innovate new ways of being in relationship with their neighbors. One of the most fascinating is the idea of "plunging."[6] Plunging is the practice of intentional relationship development with diverse neighbors through relying upon their hospitality. This often begins informally, with Christians striking up conversations with neighbors at a bus stop or some other public place. Rather than invite the neighbors to come to some event or program at church, they seek to *be* invited to accompany those neighbors to their gathering places. The primary agenda is cultivating community, listening to people's stories and dreams, and beginning to share life together.

Plunging was developed because these South African Christians did not know how to be in ministry with their neighbors. They had no credibility to sweep in and try to solve the neighbors' social problems by dispensing resources or advice—apartheid had squandered that long ago. They could not hold themselves in the superior posture of benefactors—that had created the problem in the first place. They had to become first and foremost *learners*. One Dutch Reformed megachurch actually went as far as to invite a leader from the black community to serve on its governing board without being a member of the church so that they could learn from him how to be in relationship with the black community.

Good idea

Plunging is risky, as these Christians have discovered. In one case, a small group of rather proper older white church people found themselves invited to a youth club in a black township—the kind of place they would have done everything to stay away from previously. Plunging means leaving your comfortable turf and depending upon the good will of the neighbor. It means being in places which you cannot control. South African leader Danie Mouton says:

> We do not know how to minister to those to whom we are being sent. Therefore we need to learn together with them how to minister to them, and how to receive ministry from them. By plunging into communities the invaluable bridge communities are formed that guide us forward.[7]

Plunging recognizes that God is circulating around the neighborhood, and if we want to participate in God's work of reconciling all creation, we need to learn from our neighbors how to do so.

This is a dramatic reversal of the establishment posture of many Episcopal churches. Part of the reason why so many Episcopalians feel paralyzed about reaching out in ministry to new populations (including their own children and grandchildren) is that they feel culturally incompetent. They don't know how to speak the cultural language or meet the needs of these people. The only way to overcome this is to take the risk of building community, patiently and personally. Periodic events or programs that we might try to use to invite the community to church tend to be much less effective, because they typically lack opportunity for meaningful relationships to be built, and we stay on our turf and our terms. Participation in God's mission in the world means relying upon the Spirit's leading as guests of God's hospitality, expressed through neighbors of good will.

Rethinking Public Engagement

What does all this mean for the church's role and witness in public life? As described in chapter 1, the Episcopal Church has long held a strong commitment to public advocacy and political engagement. Historically, this has tended to assume an establishment posture—that the church functions as a privileged moral authority within national life to direct the nation toward Christian values. That is no longer *a Bridge Church?*

the case. With the collapse of the national church ideal in the second half of the twentieth century, the Episcopal Church has adopted the posture of a niche church for a relatively narrow slice of the American population. It no longer has the capacity to reform the nation from the center with any real credibility. How might its public identity and engagement be reenvisioned?

Alongside Luke 10:1–12, another biblical text promises a vital alternative to the establishment approach—Jeremiah's letter to the exiles in Babylon. The elite rulers of Jerusalem had been violently displaced by King Nebuchadnezzar into exile in the foreign city of Babylon (modern-day Iraq). Against the establishment prophets and religious leaders who assumed that God's presence was focused in the Jerusalem Temple and would protect the city (and their privilege) from harm, Jeremiah tells a different story. Due to the injustice, unfaithfulness, and complacency of Jerusalem's elite, God allows a foreign empire to de-center and displace them. This was a shocking disestablishment.

Jeremiah then writes a letter to the exiles, who may have assumed that God would quickly bring them back and restore the status quo.

> Thus says the LORD of hosts, the God of Israel, to all the exiles whom I have sent into exile from Jerusalem to Babylon: Build houses and live in them; plant gardens and eat what they produce. Take wives and have sons and daughters; take wives for your sons, and give your daughters in marriage, that they may bear sons and daughters; multiply there, and do not decrease. But seek the welfare of the city where I have sent you into exile, and pray to the LORD on its behalf, for in its welfare you will find your welfare. (Jeremiah 29:4–7)

This new situation, of living amidst a foreign society as guests, rather than holding power and control back in Jerusalem, was not what they expected. They thought God would bring all nations to worship at *their* temple in Jerusalem, not that God would push them into the arms of the Babylonians. Yet Jeremiah tells them to settle in, to build community with the people in that place, to intermarry, to construct houses and plant gardens, and above all, to seek the welfare of that city. The Hebrew word translated "welfare" is *shalom*—the same thing

Jesus tells the seventy disciples to share with the villagers in Luke 10. *Shalom* means peace with justice, the reconciliation of difference into right relationships, the flourishing of the whole community. It is not mere harmony or the absence of conflict.[8]

What might it mean for Episcopal churches to recognize that the waves of change that have swept through America in the past fifty years have displaced us into a form of cultural exile? We find ourselves in an increasingly marginal position of dwelling in a pluralistic society where Christianity is merely one option among many. The Babylonian exiles had little capacity to remake the laws of Babylon from their position in society. Instead, they were told by God to indwell this reality long enough to build relationships, to seek the peace and well-being of society as guests.

Today's America is a culturally polycentric society with many religious and ethnic communities coexisting—sometimes peacefully, sometimes not. The great British missiologist Lesslie Newbigin drew a distinction that is important for us to recognize—the difference between the *fact of plurality* (a religiously and culturally diverse society) and the *ideology of pluralism* (the modern secularist belief that no religion can lay claim to ultimate truth).[9] There is no denying the fact of plurality in American life today. Yet this does not mean embracing the ideology of pluralism, which would negate the public truth claims of all religions. Episcopalians—like other American Christians—have an important voice and presence to contribute to the public conversation.

> Disestablishment invites a new form of public engagement that depends instead upon our lived identity as disciples of Jesus rather than a privileged social location.

Yet we must speak with a new humility, as a minority voice from the edges, rather than continuing to pretend we stand at the center and expect to be heard. We must no longer rely primarily upon social, cultural, political, or economic prominence to exercise influence. Disestablishment invites a new form of public engagement that depends instead upon our lived identity as disciples of Jesus rather than a privileged social location.[10] James Davison Hunter uses the phrase *faithful presence* to describe this form of engagement— being present faithfully to God in worship, to each other, to the tasks

speak [with] humility - a voice from the edges as a minority

and vocations God has given each of us to do, and within our spheres of relational influence.[11] It is a much more organic, grassroots kind of partnership in local neighborhoods and cities than we have often imagined for ourselves in the past. Yet that is where Jesus conducted his ministry—within local towns and villages—and the early church grew through relational networks. It mandates a vital and lived practice of discipleship in order for us to have something to offer. Such a practice necessarily involves distinction from the surrounding society, yet continual engagement.

In relating to members of our surrounding communities who profess different faiths, we must go in a posture of humility and mutuality. Interfaith engagement calls forth from us an invitation to understand our own tradition more deeply as we learn about our neighbor's. Our boldness in witnessing must not be the imperial boldness of establishment, but rather the very different boldness of confessing a crucified Christ. With the cross at its heart, the Christian story is peculiar and strange. It has always been that way—"a stumbling block to Jews and foolishness to the Greeks" (1 Corinthians 1:23). Yet the power of that story is rooted in the embodied witness of those who share it—their lives as well as their words. We can only confess a crucified Christ faithfully when we go in weakness, not power; when we engage people on their cultural turf, not just ours; when we listen as well as speak; when we serve others as Christ has served us.

Cultivating Growth

Remember St. James, Great Barrington, the church that now meets in the bar? The Christmas after the wall fell and they were displaced from their building, some of the church's children visited a local farm and greenhouse to make wreaths. At the farm, a conversation ensued among the children about having a garden to feed hungry people in the neighborhood. The owners of the farm offered three-quarters of an acre there for the children to cultivate and give the food away. Over time, as the children and adults worked in tending the garden, they began to strike up relationships with the migrant workers at the farm, whose children also joined in. Other neighbors from the community have since come together to cultivate the acreage (which has now expanded), and church members and neighbors work alongside one another. The food is taken weekly to a community meal site for the hungry, where the children go to talk with the people receiving it. Neighbors from the community, including the migrant workers, have been teaching the children and adults from the church about how to grow things. Children from the church have been sharing about their passion for feeding the hungry, which is rooted in the gospel. The learning has been mutual. And it has all taken place on someone else's land, a neighbor of good will who has graciously hosted them.

When Hurricane Irene brought flooding to New England in 2011, the farm's crops were devastated. Without this income, the farm owners could not purchase the Christmas trees and greens they depended upon to get through the winter. Members of the church took up a collection and secured the money to allow the farm to stay in business. The giving goes both ways. St. James's rector, Francie Hills, says, "What goes on in that garden is church."

Questions for Discussion

1. Share a story of a time when you received or depended upon the hospitality of strangers. What did it feel like? What happened there?

2. Has your church ever gone into its surrounding community to share the peace with neighbors without carrying baggage or resources? What might it mean to do so?

3. How might your church "seek the peace of the city" in your local community? What kind of public presence does it currently have, and what kind of presence might God be calling you to?

CHAPTER 6

A PEOPLE . . .

Living as Disciples

For Christians are not differentiated from other people by country, language, or customs; you see, they do not live in cities of their own, or speak some strange dialect, or have some peculiar lifestyle. This teaching of theirs has not been contrived by the invention and speculation of inquisitive men. Nor are they propagating mere human teaching as some people do. They live in both Greek and foreign cities, wherever chance has put them. They follow local customs in clothing, food, and the other aspects of life. But at the same time, they demonstrate to us the wonderful and certainly unusual form of their own citizenship. They live in their own native lands, but as aliens; as citizens, they share all things with others; but like aliens, suffer all things. Every foreign country is to them as their native country, and every native land as a foreign country. They marry and have children just like everyone else; but they do not kill unwanted babies. They offer a shared table, but not a shared bed. They are at present "in the flesh" but they do not live "according to the flesh." They are passing their days on earth, but are citizens of heaven. They obey the appointed laws, and go beyond the laws in their own lives. They love everyone, but are persecuted by all. They are unknown and condemned; they are put to death and gain life. They are poor and yet make many rich. They are short of everything and yet have plenty of all things. They are dishonored and yet gain glory through dishonor. . . . Christians are in the world but not of the world.[1]

This anonymous letter, possibly written in the second century, describes the distinctive identity of followers of Jesus in a society at times indifferent, hostile, and curious about their way of life. Christians participate in ordinary life in society yet do so uniquely, with different ultimate allegiances and practices. Their conduct is exemplary. Their life points beyond themselves to a heavenly citizenship, which gives them their true identity, yet also calls them to share in the struggles and suffering of the world.

The sociologist Rodney Stark describes how the early church grew within the relational networks of the Mediterranean world by living as a community of compassion that attracted attention from its surrounding neighbors.[2] For instance, when epidemics swept through the claustrophobic and unsanitary cities, most everyone fled, except the sick, aged, and poor, who couldn't—and the Christians who stayed behind to care for them.

> Renewing Episcopal identity after the era of establishment involves recovering deeper theological and spiritual roots.

Christians rescued and raised unwanted infants—often girls—exposed to die outside of towns and villages. When persecutions came, the steadfast faith of Christians in the face of torture and death drew notice. People wondered what belief could motivate people to give up so much in order to stay true to it. In a world of deep social inequality, class division, military violence, and economic oppression, the way of life of the Christian community offered a compelling alternative of equality, mutual care-giving, reconciliation, and service toward the neighbor.

For Episcopalians, the legacy of establishment long ago eroded any clear sense of distinctiveness from the surrounding society. Within what was assumed to be a functionally Christian society, Episcopalians found their uniqueness in their privileged socioeconomic status, in the aesthetic refinement of their worship (the two are not unrelated), and in their sense of incorporating the best of the various Christian traditions into one whole (the "national church" ideal). Membership in the church was not based upon exhibiting a way of life that called into question the values of the dominant culture, but rather more typically reflected one's high standing within that culture.

There was assumed to be little need to distinguish heavenly citizenship from earthly citizenship, for Christian identity was thought to pervade society.

Renewing Episcopal identity after the era of establishment involves recovering deeper theological and spiritual roots—a sense of the church as a community of the Way of Jesus sent to participate in God's mission of reconciling all creation. We need to discover what it might mean for us to claim the identity of *disciples*, not mere members of an institutional church, in ways that resonate with our values, commitments, and gifts. The vitality of our identity as the church depends upon the vitality of our discipleship, which in the era of functional establishment tended to be underdeveloped. Now is the time to renew our understanding of what it means to live as people of the Way of Jesus in relationship to a society that is at times indifferent, hostile, and curious.

The Baptismal Covenant: Defining Discipleship

As described in chapters 3 and 4, the Spirit reconciles and draws us into new community in Christ in the sacrament of baptism. That community experiences God's grace and healing in the Eucharist, where the brokenness of our lives and the world is transformed into a foretaste of the heavenly feast. Christian ministry begins in baptism, where our identities are changed and we live no longer for ourselves, but for God, for one another, and for our neighbors in the world. We become participating members of the body of Christ through the power of the Spirit.

The Book of Common Prayer contains a rich description of what the life of ministry for all of the baptized looks like in the baptismal covenant (pages 304–5). This blueprint for Christian discipleship is worth reflecting upon as we explore further what it means to be people of the Way of Jesus in today's world. In the liturgy, the baptismal covenant begins with the Apostles' Creed, the ancient baptismal confession that affirms the doctrines of the Trinity and incarnation that are unique to Christianity. To each question, the people affirm "I will, with God's help." This acknowledges two important realities: that discipleship involves active commitment on our part, and that without God's agency and assistance, we will fail. Let's unpack each question in more detail.

Will you continue in the apostles' teaching and fellowship, in the breaking of bread, and in the prayers?

This statement echoes Acts 2:46, where the new community created at Pentecost shares in a powerful experience gathered around communal prayer, meals, and the teaching of the apostles. Within the baptismal covenant, it recognizes the importance of participation in communal worship, where we learn the stories that shape our unique identity, where we receive God's hospitality in the Eucharist and share meals together, and where we experience a life of prayer. The elements of this statement are intentionally expansive—they could take place anywhere, not just in traditional Sunday worship. There are many forms of community life that are encompassed by these activities.

Continuing in the apostles' teaching is a central challenge for many Episcopalians. As with many mainline denominations, the Bible tends to be underutilized within the Episcopal Church. For some, the Bible is an intimidating book that seems difficult to enter into meaningfully. Congregational leaders are often unsure how to make it accessible. There are harsh texts in the Bible that seem to exclude some people from the church's life. Many struggle to understand how to make sense of it. In some congregations, clergy have taken the role of experts who use their knowledge primarily to explain *away* the Bible's relevance. Many lay disciples end up feeling either shamed by their lack of knowledge of the Bible or ill-equipped to engage it meaningfully in their own lives of faith.

Renewing the identity of the Episcopal Church requires us to go deeper into the core narratives that shape us as a people, and those begin in the Bible. It is vital that congregations acknowledge openly that the Bible is not an easy book to make sense of—that it indeed contains challenging stories, and that we need to read it carefully and prayerfully together in community and in light of the wisdom of diverse viewpoints. Congregational leaders must find ways of helping members engage the Bible without fear of being shamed. One mainline congregation declared amnesty by offering a "Bible for Dummies" class that has proven highly popular.[3] The class makes no assumptions of prior knowledge and is aimed at empowering ordinary members to be able to read the Bible on their own as well as in community together.

Scripture must come alive in fresh ways within congregational life. Theological and spiritual renewal means cultivating God-shaped imaginations within the life of the church and all its members.

> Renewing the identity of the Episcopal Church requires us to go deeper into the core narratives that shape us as a people, and those begin in the Bible.

As described in chapter 2, the predominant ways of seeing the world and experiencing daily life within modern Western societies tend to be highly secularized. There is little capacity to imagine God actively present and at work. Many Episcopalians seem to struggle to name God's movement in their lives and world. One of the central challenges to renewing Episcopal identity today is the cultivation of theological imagination. Engaging the Bible is vital to addressing this challenge.

Many congregations around the world today have discovered the power of imaginative ways of reflecting upon scripture in community. This includes the recovery of ancient practices like Lectio Divina, African Bible Study, the Gospel-Based Discipleship approach developed by Native American Episcopalians, or Dwelling in the Word.[4] In these practices, there is no "expert" teacher upon whom congregation members must depend for answers. Rather, the text is placed within the center of the community and all are invited to engage it imaginatively and listen to God's voice through it.

The congregation I serve has found Dwelling in the Word to be incredibly transformative. In Dwelling in the Word, a brief passage of scripture (usually less than a dozen verses) is read aloud, while participants are invited to consider two questions: "Where was your imagination caught while the passage was read?" or "What question would you like to ask a biblical scholar about the text?" After a period of si-

good questions

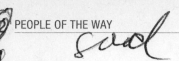

lent reflection, people are encouraged to find a partner to share with. The pairs listen attentively to one another, for when it is time to report back to the larger group, participants share not what *they* heard, but what their *partners* heard. This invites people into a posture of deep listening—to the Word and to one another—as well as forces them to advocate publically for one another's voice.

These ways of continuing in the apostles' teaching and fellowship by opening up the Bible to imaginative engagement foster a different kind of conversation within the church's life. Bible stories begin to take on a life of their own, where the scriptural narrative connects with our daily life and practice. This avoids the ways the Bible is reduced in some American congregations today, either to a rule book ("God's toolbox for right living") or a source of pious platitudes ("all the Bible really says is that God is love"). Neither of these engages the narrative integrity or complexity of the biblical witness.[5]

We can no longer assume that people know the Bible when they come to church or that the brief episodes served up in the lectionary fit together into any kind of coherent whole in people's minds. Rather what tends to happen is that bits of the Bible that make sense to people are fit into the frameworks they bring, which are shaped by the dominant secular culture. That culture is focused on what Miroslav Volf calls "experiential satisfaction," not on Christian discipleship.[6] The parts that don't fit are simply jettisoned or ignored. The wider coherence of the biblical story (with all its strangeness and complexity) fails to take hold. In order for theological renewal and deeper discipleship to take place, the Bible must become the primary framework by which people make sense out of their lives and the surrounding culture, instead of the reverse. This requires intentionality on the part of congregational leaders to innovate creative ways through which the Bible can come alive for congregation members.

Will you persevere in resisting evil, and, whenever you fall into sin, repent and return to the Lord?

The call to Christian discipleship is a call to conversion—deep change that encompasses our hearts, minds, and every aspect of our lives.

This part of the baptismal covenant acknowledges the persistent reality of evil and sin (the breaking of community) in the world and the need for disciples to live lives of resistance and repentance. One of the myths of modern Western culture is that evil is simply ignorance—with the right education, it can be overcome. This myth has fueled optimism in technological progress as the means to resolve all human problems and unify the planet. Instead, the past hundred years have demonstrated how technology can fuel some of the most horrifying genocides in human history, undertaken by highly educated people. Evil and sin remain very much with us.

> Resisting evil and practicing repentance offer a compelling alternative to a culture of superficiality.

One of the gifts of the Anglican tradition is a Reformed stream that deeply shaped the thought of Thomas Cranmer and the theology of the Book of Common Prayer. This stream has never been shy about naming the human tendency toward evil and its capacity to corrupt ourselves, the church, and the world. Against naïve optimism about human self-perfection, we must recognize our continual need for repentance and renewal, for God's healing grace. Living as Christian disciples means attending to the power of evil in the world, which breaks community, estranges people from God, one another, and the earth, and fosters injustice and oppression. We must name that power while always recognizing we are implicated in it—that the church as a human community is always imperfect and liable to distort the gospel.

Living as people of the Way means recognizing our continual propensity to choose wrongly, to seek our own selfish ends, and to fail in our efforts to live as faithful people. One of the reasons for hesitancy about sharing the gospel among Episcopalians and other mainline Protestants is a sense of guilt over the church's failures and shortcomings. We are embarrassed by the Crusades and other ways in which Christians have abused power in the name of Jesus, and rightly so. Yet the response is sometimes to diminish the depth of the gospel by minimizing the discussion of sin and evil and our participation in it. The gospel becomes a kind of self-help guide or optimistic program for social improvement. Reclaiming a vital and bold witness requires us to acknowledge regularly and openly our sinfulness while always at the same time confessing God's gracious and transformational response. Many people in today's world are seeking authentic community, which mandates candor about ourselves, our life together, and the broken world in which we live. Resisting evil and practicing repentance offer a compelling alternative to a culture of superficiality.

Will you proclaim by word and example the Good News of God in Christ?

Episcopalians tend to struggle with evangelism. There are multiple reasons for this: the assumption that it means coercive proselytizing;

> Evangelism is "that set of intentional activities which is governed by the goal of initiating people in the kingdom of God for the first time."

modern culture's relegation of faith to a matter of private individual choice; establishment assumptions about the society already being somehow Christian; anemic discipleship; or a lack of clarity about what the Good News of God in Christ really is for us. Often, the conversation around evangelism is reduced to new-member recruitment. The baptismal covenant's description of a holistic approach ("by word *and* example") is limited to "an evangelism of deeds" where the story of Jesus is never told, or vice versa—verbal proclamation fails to be integrated with service and life witness.

It's time to renew our understanding and practice of evangelism and proclamation. We might begin by invoking a *theological* definition of evangelism as "that set of intentional activities which is governed by the goal of initiating people in the kingdom of God for the first time."[7] What we are proclaiming by word and example is the coming of God's reign in Jesus, which addresses every aspect of life. God's reign is the reconciliation of people with God and one another, the forgiveness of sins, the healing of wounds, the liberation of the enslaved, and the reordering of human community in just and merciful ways. It is cosmic in scope, both personal and public. It is present in part and yet to be fully revealed.

Intentionally initiating people into the reign of God requires a holistic approach—opening up experiences of that reign and interpreting them with people in light of the biblical story. It mandates sensitive attention to the contexts in which people live today. Merely explaining what Jesus taught about the reign of God without offering some lived taste of it doesn't go far enough. As Lesslie Newbigin observes, we only know God's forgiveness through the concrete word and gesture of other human beings.[8] The church's communal life—both as brought into focus in the sacraments of baptism and Eucharist and in the daily witness and ministry of disciples in the world—offers a tangible, visible sign of God's reign. It is a flawed and imperfect sign that should never be equated fully with the reign, but it is a real sign nonetheless.

The missiologist Craig Van Gelder likens the church to a demonstration plot on a farm.[9] Demonstration plots are small sections on the edge of a farm in public view where new farming methods, seeds, or fertilizers are used. Farmers watch this plot attentively before deciding to commit to using the new methods or materials on their own fields. Sometimes, things don't always go perfectly. But the demonstration plot offers a concrete, lived witness to an alternative to the status quo. The church is God's demonstration plot for human community, where we are called and shaped by the Holy Spirit to offer in our life a different vision for human flourishing. That vision is credible precisely because the struggles and sinfulness of humanity are acknowledged and dealt with through God's grace and the practices of forgiveness and reconciliation. It must be interpreted to those outside if it is to have any value.

In a postestablishment era, proclamation and evangelism must be conducted in a posture of humility, mutual vulnerability, and dialogue. The church lost a great deal of credibility through its identification with political, economic, and cultural power. It cannot perpetuate those imperial patterns if it is to speak and be heard in today's context. What is required is the formation of relationships and community, largely on the neighbor's turf, where stories can be heard on all sides. We must begin with a posture of attentive listening. Episcopalians will have to learn to tell their own stories of faith. Congregation members can begin by practicing with one another. As those conversa-

The church · God's demonstration plot.

tions unfold with neighbors, there is often a time where it is fitting to invite our neighbors to dwell imaginatively with us in the rich and provocative metaphors and parables Jesus uses or other stories from scripture. What they hear in those stories is as important as what we might tell them. Having learned to listen to God's Word together in our own communities, we can then learn to listen to our neighbors and to what God might be saying to and through them.

Will you seek and serve Christ in all persons, loving your neighbor as yourself?

This question of the baptismal covenant brings into focus the importance of loving our neighbors as Christ has loved us, recognizing that Christ comes to us as the stranger or guest. The doctrine of the incarnation represents God's *yes* to human life—a critical affirmation of ordinary life and cultures. In the incarnation, God does not merely bless things as they are in their fallen, distorted state, but rather corrects and heals what has been broken and points the way toward new and abundant life. This changes our view toward our neighbors in the world. We cannot separate people into categories of the worthy and worthless as our culture would have us do, for Christ has given his life for all. Every person has God-given *intrinsic* value, not just instrumental value for what she or he can provide to us. We cannot understand Christ more fully without coming to know our neighbors, in whom the image of God is present.

> Seeking Christ means discerning how God is alive and at work within our neighborhoods and in the lives of our neighbors.

Seeking Christ means discerning how God is alive and at work within our neighborhoods and in the lives of our neighbors. The practice of discernment is vitally important if churches are to participate in God's mission of reconciliation in their times and places. It addresses the central question of what God might be up to—a question we must always approach with great humility. For in the gospels, the disciples are often confused about who Jesus is and what his ministry is all about, and we sometimes fare no better. Yet that doesn't disqualify us from asking this question prayerfully and attentively.

In many Episcopal congregations, the term "discernment" is associated with episodic, extraordinary activities. For instance, those sensing a call to ordination enter a special discernment process. Congregations often try to discern their identity and gifts when preparing to call a new rector, or discernment precedes the launching of a capital campaign. But discernment must be a *way of life* for Christian disciples and Christian communities seeking to participate in God's reign. It is a cultivated capacity for attending to God's presence and movement—for seeking and serving Christ through the Spirit.

St. Matthew's Episcopal Church in St. Paul, Minnesota, embarked upon a creative discernment process a few years ago focused on identifying the future that God was bringing forth for the congregation. The church wondered about how its gifts could contribute to God's mission in its time and place. Since asking this question directly often leads to blank stares or merely pragmatic answers, the leaders of the process approached the question indirectly—through prayerful play and imaginative exercises. For instance, the hospitality ministry was asked to come up with a menu that represented the future God was bringing forth. People were invited in small groups to build depictions of that future out of Legos or to paint pictures of it. The process was framed by Dwelling in the Word. Rich stories and images were evoked and interpreted along the way.

At the conclusion of the process, one vestry member known for his sharp intellect stood up at the annual meeting and said that previously, he dreaded "discernment" because it always seemed directed toward problem-solving or some predetermined end. But what he realized now is that it is really a process of *wondering*—prayerfully attending in a posture of wonder, awe, and curiosity to God's presence and movement in our midst and beyond.

There is an old missionary adage that when missionaries enter a new culture or town, they should remove their shoes, for they are standing on holy ground. God always goes before us in mission and is present through creation, the incarnation, and the Spirit in the lives of the neighbors to whom we are sent. In a society of perpetual technological distraction, fickle tastes, and shifting allegiances, cultivating

Creative discernment - a process of wondering

a community of wonder takes patience, discipline, and intentionality. It calls us to practice the deep spiritual disciplines that have shaped Christian life for centuries, such as prayer, silence, Sabbath, service, simplicity, generosity, hospitality, worship, and solitude. Our ability to serve and love our neighbor faithfully depends upon our ability to recognize Christ in her or him, which means receiving as well as giving. The Christian life should be a life of wonder.

Will you strive for justice and peace among all people, and respect the dignity of every human being?

As we discern the Spirit's movement in our midst and in the world around us, we are caught up in God's mission of restoring human community to right relationships. Living as people of the Way means sharing in Christ's compassion for the vulnerable, suffering, hungry, homeless, and poor. Membership in the body of Christ is a call to bring our spiritual and material gifts to bear upon the injustices and conflicts in our neighborhoods, nation, and the world. We do so as participants in God's reign of justice and mercy, not because we can solve the world's problems through our own strength. The restoration of human community is primarily God's work in which we share. We find our identity as recipients of God's mercy and meaningful collaborators in God's mission. We are freed *from* slavery to sin and evil in order to live *for* our neighbors in love.

This means that we must learn to have eyes to see the in-breaking of that reign within our world, including naming the places and ways in which it is inhibited by the powers of evil and sin. In order to discern the reign of God, we must attend carefully to the biblical narrative and recognize that sometimes we are the very ones obstructing that reign. To be human is to be entrusted with stewardship over human life and the earth in God's image (Genesis 1:28). This means creative, collaborative care, not exploitation and violence. It involves seeking the flourishing of all people, not just the privileged few.

Striving for justice and peace is costly. Jesus lost his life for it. We can expect resistance as well, for it calls us to differentiate ourselves from powerful patterns in our globalized economy and culture. Late-modern global capitalism has created incredible wealth for many around the world (including many Episcopalians), yet far greater numbers are impoverished and exploited. We live in a time of economic displacement and uncertainty. Government at various levels is breaking down in mistrust, acrimony, and dysfunction in the face of massive challenges. There is no clear consensus in America about how to pursue the common good, and in today's media environment, citizens increasingly talk past one another.

The church has a vital calling in the midst of this world as a community of compassion, conversation, and hope. The Way of Jesus provides a stark alternative to the predominant ways of construing human meaning, purpose, and community in our society. Jesus rejected the "lording over" commonplace within his society and ours in favor of sharing power sacrificially with others. He did not hold himself aloof, but was willing to humiliate himself in order to serve his followers. Rather than perpetuate the cycles of violence and retribution that characterize so much of human history, he broke them by absorbing conflict into his own body. To those too attached to their wealth and status to share community with the poor and dispossessed, he called them to a new life of open hearts and hands.

> Living as disciples means following the energy of the Holy Spirit as it moves in the midst of our churches and neighborhoods, creating and restoring community, challenging patterns of injustice, and bringing peace.

Living as disciples means following the energy of the Holy Spirit as it moves in the midst of our churches and neighborhoods, creating and restoring community, challenging patterns of injustice, and bringing peace. Many church leaders today find themselves weary from feeling like they need to bring the energy to catalyze people into action or engagement. Church committees and ministry teams sometimes sag under the purposelessness and inertia of doing what has always been done. Attending to the Spirit in a posture of wonder and expectation changes things. We are freed to let go of forms of ministry that no longer serve God's mission. We are swept up into the Spirit's creativity as new expressions of ministry emerge. Leaders can shift their focus from trying to engage, entertain, or appease con-

wonder + Expectation → change

gregation members and instead help those members identify and interpret the Spirit's work in their daily lives. This includes discerning their spiritual gifts and callings. It is a far more adventurous and meaningful journey in which to participate.

Anglicanism's Gifts for Twenty-First-Century America

How are Episcopalians and other Anglicans uniquely shaped to contribute to God's mission in today's U.S. context? What does God want from the Episcopal Church and other Anglican expressions today? Reflecting on these questions is vital to claiming a positive identity. Far too many times, I have heard Episcopalians describe themselves by what they are *not*—not fundamentalist, not Roman Catholic, etc. Now is the time to claim what we *do* have to offer the many people in our neighborhoods searching to find meaning, purpose, healing, and community. *a Bridge To God.*

we have the freedom,

Cultural Translation

As described in chapter 1 above, Anglicanism has a national and contextual character—it engages, reflects, and adapts to the particular cultural and social settings in which it finds itself.[10] Unlike some Protestant traditions, which are normed to confessions developed in historical settings very different from our own (sixteenth-century Europe, for instance), Anglicanism has a great degree of freedom to change dynamically as the context changes. This freedom accounts in part for the vitality of global Anglicanism today, as Anglican Christians around the world have adapted the tradition in light of their own cultural situations. It has fostered the diversity and complexity of the Anglican Communion, as well as some of its conflicts.

> Far too many times, I have heard Episcopalians describe themselves by what they are *not*—not fundamentalist, not Roman Catholic, etc. Now is the time to claim what we *do* have to offer.

This commitment to cultural translation challenges us to participate in the reshaping of Episcopal Church life to reflect a changing America. Contextualization of the gospel and church does not mean uncritical embrace of or accommodation to the surrounding culture. Rather, it is a deeper process of engagement in which the gospel takes root in changing language and cultural forms in order to speak to people in their native tongues. As Lesslie Newbigin observes, "There can never be a culture-free gospel. Yet the gospel, which is from the beginning to the end embodied in culturally conditioned forms, calls into question all cultures, including the one in which it was originally embodied."[11]

What does this freedom to adapt and reinterpret the church's life and witness mean for us? It is an invitation to recognize the diversity of cultures present within American life today and to empower the church to renew its witness through translating its life to reflect that diversity. Deep in our Reformation heritage is the vernacular principle—that worship should be in the language of the people. The Book of Common Prayer is one of the greatest expressions of that principle in Christian history. The vernacular principle means that our liturgies and common life must continue to be adapted and translated as the languages and cultures in our nation change. The question the church must ask itself is, "Are we worshipping in the language of the people, or are we asking them to worship in a foreign tongue?" This doesn't apply only to immigrants whose first language is not English. It also applies to younger generations and newcomers to church who need expressions of Episcopal worship and life that resonate with their native ways of speaking and being together.

Contextualization means that the church's life is necessarily dynamic as local disciples innovate new forms of Christian witness under the leadership of the Spirit in order to speak to new populations. Contrary to what seems to be the assumption of many congregations, change and adaptation are integral to our DNA as a church. Critical and transformational embrace of local cultures is how the church speaks to a changing world. Considering how central the incarnation is to Anglican theology, I've always found it ironic that Episcopal churches can be so resistant to change. Incarnation means translation and adaptation. Without it, we're only speaking to those already inside the circle, and there is no future in that.

Liturgical Worship in an Image-Based Age

For much of the modern period, Western culture was word-based. This reflects the powerful changes brought about by the invention of the printing press and the growth in literacy beginning in the fifteenth century. The churches of the Reformation, including Anglicanism, shifted from the primarily visual, dramatic, and tactile way of communicating in the medieval church to a spoken and written one. Many Episcopalians today would be surprised at how spare Anglican worship tended to be from the English Reformation through the mid-nineteenth century. It was a church of the word, focused on the words of the Prayer Book, the words of sermons, and the recitation of psalms, with hymns to accompany it all.

A significant shift is taking place today, however, from a word-based to an image-based culture. The rise of film, television, the Internet, mobile devices, and social media have fostered this change, together with the ubiquity of advertising. No longer do most people take the time to write letters to one another; instead, they text or post pictures on Facebook. Instead of reading newspapers, people watch YouTube or check Twitter on their phones or tablets. We're now used to accessing pictures and graphic images of anything imaginable from anywhere, anytime. Younger generations who are natives to this digital culture are leading the way.

What this means for the church is that the visual dimension of worship is critically important for communicating in today's world. Asking people to sit on hard pews to listen primarily to an hour's worth of words (whether in the liturgy or sermons) takes them out of their native culture. They are accustomed instead to a rich variety of mediated images which they expect to help shape and interact with in today's participatory media culture. How might Christianity speak within this culture?

Of all the Christian traditions, Episcopalians and other Anglicans are perhaps best positioned for this shift. Worship in our churches tends to value multiple means of artistic expression—the drama of the liturgy, colorful vestments and church decorations, icons, paintings, candles, movement, music, the tangible experience of sharing in the bread and wine, even incense. The story is being told in images as well as in words—and the words remain critically important. There is a reverence for and expression of mystery in Episcopal worship not always found elsewhere. Many evangelical churches are highly creative at using new media, and we can learn from them about how to incorporate this dimension into our worship, yet that use is often instrumental toward a predetermined end. Episcopal worship generally seeks not just to move people toward a particular decision or stir a certain feeling, but rather to enter a rich experience of transcendence, a taste of heaven. The dangers are always clericalism and mystification, when the experience is too tightly controlled by the few and the rest don't understand it.

The sociologist David Roozen found in a study of denominations that liturgical and charismatic traditions are best at adapting to the emerging postmodern culture. In contrast, what he termed "more Calvinist or cognitive" denominations had a harder time.[12] There is a new emphasis on spiritual experience in the emerging postmodern culture which both liturgical and charismatic expressions of church speak to in ways that more rationalistic ones do not. This emphasis appeals not just to people in postmodern culture, but also to many immigrant cultures. Those cultures are typically less shaped by Enlightenment modernity, with its rationalism. People expect religion to embody and celebrate the mystical, experiential, visual, and tactile.

Episcopal worship embraces ancient elements, which provides a depth and rootedness that is increasingly appealing to people adrift in a culture of the new and the next. As the pace of cultural change increases in twenty-first-century society, many people yearn for more stable anchors of wisdom and meaning. The phenomenon of younger evangelicals moving into Anglicanism is an expression of this as they seek to participate and worship in churches steeped in ancient traditions and history.[13] There is also the danger of traditionalism, as some churches resist adapting and opening up the riches of their traditions to new generations and populations as a way of reacting to cultural changes they cannot control.

The challenge and opportunity for Episcopalians is to retain the depth and richness of our legacy while creatively rendering it accessible to newcomers. This happens best in collaboration with those newcomers as they are apprenticed into the disciplines and wisdom of the community and at the same time encouraged to reinterpret them in new vernaculars. Episcopalians tend to value the arts and creativity. This stems in part from our emphasis on incarnation—God's presence and witness through human life and culture. Yet that emphasis is often too narrowly conceived. Churches sometimes try to imitate English cathedral worship of times long past rather than discovering how the richness of that cultural legacy can speak afresh in today's cultures. This is a matter of local discernment through the Spirit and in cooperation with new generations and populations. It requires the opening up of power over congregational life by those accustomed to holding it. We are called to interpret and adapt the richness of our worship and communal life without reducing it in the name of a superficial sense of relevance.

Theological Breadth and Diversity

> The historic Anglican tolerance for complexity and ambiguity is a gift in a postmodern world, where paradox, ambiguity, and mystery are valued, not explained away.

Anglicanism is remarkable for its theological breadth, drawing expansively on sources across the centuries and streams of Christian tradition. Historically, this has been known as "comprehension"—the idea that Anglicanism can span Catholic, Protestant, and Eastern Orthodox teachings, values, and commitments within one whole. Such expansiveness can come at the expense of clarity and coherence. Yet it also has a powerful upside—the ability to encourage and tolerate diversity of thought and practice in a diverse society.

During the period of modernity, there was a strong emphasis on uniformity and universality as Westerners assumed their culture was the world's best and that all other cultures needed to be "developed" along its lines. In the past fifty years, such assumptions have been called deeply into question. There is a new affirmation of difference. Moreover, many people in today's emerging postmodern culture are restless with merely accepting what their parents or grandparents believed and practiced. They want to participate in creating meaning and community, often out of a variety of diverse sources, rather than simply accepting what is handed to them. One of the primary reasons young adults leave church in America is that their questions and doubts aren't tolerated.[14] The Episcopal Church offers space to wrestle, to question, to wonder in community together. Episcopalians tend to have an open posture toward insights from science and other fields of human inquiry.

Within the framework of the historic creeds, the Prayer Book, and an ordered ministry, Anglicanism offers remarkable freedom. As discussed earlier, under the influence of modern Western individualism, that freedom can devolve into fragmentation and a loss of Christian identity. But positively, it can offer a richness of Christian witness and practice that one would be hard pressed to find elsewhere. The historic Anglican tolerance for complexity and ambiguity is a gift in a postmodern world, where paradox, ambiguity, and mystery are valued, not explained away. Given how deeply shaped by modernist assumptions so many other Christian traditions are, Anglicanism has space for a different kind of knowing and practicing of the faith.

The Benedictine Legacy: A School for God's Service

Such knowledge and practice of the faith work best when shaped by deep and intentional patterns of community life. A rich Benedictine heritage underlies the Prayer Book and Anglican ideas of community (reflected in the Daily Office and the weekly forms of ordered worship). This tradition sees intentional community as integral to growth in Christian discipleship. St. Benedict described the monastery as "a school for God's service."[15] By sharing a life of stability, simplicity, common worship, hospitality, and labor, we increase in our capacity to love God and others. The wisdom of Benedict and the monastic tradition is that spiritual growth happens best within a disciplined and ordered communal life, where some freedoms are renounced so that greater spiritual freedom can be realized. In today's society, where people relocate frequently (sometimes out of economic necessity, sometimes in pursuit of new or more varied experiences), the Benedictine legacy points toward the wisdom of committing to a place—a worshipping community and a neighborhood in which to cultivate meaningful relationships. The postestablishment paradigm of mission suggested in this book requires the forming of relationships with neighbors that go beyond the surface. This involves a commitment to stability.

Several years ago, the church where I currently serve held a series of table conversations focused on the primary challenges congregation members had identified as facing them and their families, as well as our surrounding community. One of these was *family*—a recognition that many people lived apart from their extended families, and that the relationships of mutual support, mentoring, and love that have characterized human life for so many generations were being uprooted in today's mobile society. At this table, some of the American members shared how deeply they craved stable, intergenerational community in the face of today's patterns of dislocation and isolation. A church member from Kenya admitted his astonishment at how American life was organized, sharing how in his culture, the village provides that kind of supportive community. Your village identity is primary, and the sense of belonging goes deep, in part because people don't move around as often.

They began to wonder together about how the church might become that kind of village for people in contemporary America—a place of intergenerational sharing, mentoring, and mutual support. While it was recognized that some people would have to leave from time to time and others would join, what if there was a commitment among the majority to make this community primary? What if we vowed to be there to help raise one another's children, to care for our elders, to accept and be patient with the people who annoy us, to allow the relationships to go deep?[16]

This vision taps into the wisdom of the Benedictine heritage in Anglicanism, which values community, stability, intentionality, and service. Interestingly, during the flourishing of monasticism in medieval Europe, the primary missionaries were monks and nuns freed and

They will celebrate.

motivated by the disciplines of their life together to cross boundaries and create new community. Europe was evangelized by the monastic movement, and local monasteries served as vital centers of aid to the poor, education, and hospitality.[17] If, as Richard Foster has suggested, "superficiality is the curse of our age,"[18] the Episcopal Church can offer relatively stable, ordered patterns of community life that allow people to live deeply together, even without taking monastic vows. It is fascinating to watch new forms of lay monasticism arise today, such as the Order of Mission (started at St. Thomas' Church, Crookes in Sheffield, England) or the various experiments in new monastic communities being formed among younger generations.[19]

Living as People of the Way

Renewing the identity of Episcopalians in the U.S. involves the intentional formation of Christian disciples in community. The church once large-ly assumed families or the surrounding culture shouldered responsibility for that task (or at least strongly supported the church in its efforts to do

> Rather than assuming we have everything figured out and under control (the establishment attitude), we must embrace the identity of learners, even when learning entails failure.

so). Today, developing Christian disciples must become the church's first order of business. Without renewed discipleship, it's hard to see how the church can offer much that's distinctive to its neighbors. It's hard to envision much of a future.

Fortunately, the Anglican tradition offers rich resources with which to meet this challenge. The Prayer Book includes a robust vision for the shape of Christian life and ministry in the baptismal covenant. We have unique gifts to contribute to the church and so-ciety. What is required is a new kind of posture, one of learning, in-novation, experimentation, and discovery. Rather than assuming we have everything figured out and under control (the establishment at-titude), we must embrace the identity of learners, even when learning entails failure. Out of those failures (if we reflect upon them) comes growth. After all, to be a disciple is to be a learner. The alternative is a different, much more catastrophic kind of failure—the failure to pass

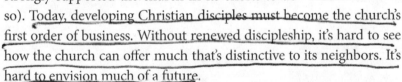

The identity of learners

on a vibrant faith to new generations and populations and to live into our identity as participants in God's ongoing mission of creating and restoring community in Christ.

Questions for
Discussion

1. Which parts of the baptismal covenant resonate most with you? Which do you find most challenging or difficult to live into?

2. How would you positively define Anglicanism's gifts for your local community? What do you see as the most precious treasures we have to offer our neighbors?

3. What does it mean to embrace the identity of learners of the Way of Jesus? How might focusing on this affect your church's life and ministry?

CHAPTER 7

A PEOPLE . . .

Organized for Mission

St. David's Episcopal Church in Ashburn, Virginia, was started in 1990 with a dozen people and a small piece of land upon which the ruins of a nineteenth-century Episcopal chapel stood. All around, what had been farmland for centuries was being rapidly transformed into suburbs of greater metropolitan Washington, DC. As the congregation grew through outreach into the burgeoning new community, many traditional elements of Episcopal life were retained—a classic (though Spirit-filled) approach to Prayer Book liturgy, a bustling Sunday school for children, a robed choir. When it came time to build the sanctuary, however, a rather unusual feature was placed prominently in the center aisle: a full-immersion baptistery, decorated with mosaic tiles like early Byzantine baptisteries.

This baptistery signified the church's new apostolic context, as the great majority of the surrounding neighbors had no church affiliation. Adult baptisms were common. The congregation experimented with creative forms of worship, such as a bluegrass and old-time gospel service on Sunday evenings that drew people from far and wide. It also developed a rather unusual approach to leadership. Rather than the establishment model of hiring one priest for every 150 members (the number of relationships that one person can typically maintain), there was one full-time priest for over 1,500 members. He concentrated on his gift areas of presiding in worship, preaching, and pastoral care. Everything else was handled by lay leaders, some on staff but mostly volunteers. Several of the key staff were in fact volunteers, invited to use their gifts to contribute to the church's leadership and given a computer and office. A small-group structure and intentional development fostered a leadership multiplication culture, where ministry authority was shared widely. With little establishment baggage, St. David's felt free to adapt creatively in its organization and common life to its missionary situation.

Organized for Establishment

The Episcopal Church remains largely organized for the world of establishment, however. Most Episcopal congregations were planted many decades or even centuries ago, in very different cultural contexts. The norms and assumptions of those contexts continue to affect the church's functioning and patterns of organization. One of the church's challenges throughout the ages has been to adapt its organization to changing cultural circumstances. This is a major issue for the Episcopal Church today and the focus of this chapter.[1]

Church organization is always contextual. That is, it reflects the cultural setting in which the body of Christ is incarnate within specific times and places. Anglicanism has historically embraced this reality through its national character—engaging and taking root within the particular cultural features of England and then every other nation in which it has found itself. Richard Hooker, the key early interpreter of Anglican polity, affirmed the dynamic character of church organization:

> There is no reason in the world wherefore we should esteem it as necessary always to do, as always to believe, the same things; seeing every man knoweth that the matter of faith is constant, the matter contrariwise of action daily changeable, especially the matter of action belonging unto church polity.[2]

William White, the architect of the democratic reorganization of the church after the American Revolution, similarly saw organization-

The Church's organization — and its ecclesiology → part of its incarnation (handwritten annotation)

al structures as dependent upon changing circumstances.[3] Like Hooker, he upheld the historic pattern of leadership offices inherited from the church's first several centuries (bishops, priests, and deacons) while adapting it to include greater lay participation and democracy.

How the church is organized not only carries cultural assumptions; it also reflects theological ones too. What kind of image of God is reflected in how the church is organized and led? While this question is often not widely discussed, it is important to ponder, for the church's organization must embody its identity. This is part of its incarnational character. This book has argued that today's changed missionary context in the United States calls us to rediscover the church's identity in the triune God's life and love for the world, rather than in cultural establishment. What does this mean for organizing the church for mission today? In order to answer this question, we must first identify some of the ways in which establishment assumptions continue to influence the organization of the Episcopal Church.

> What kind of image of God is reflected in how the church is organized and led? *Communal Trinitarian God* (handwritten annotation)

The State Church Legacy

As noted in chapter 1, the rise of Christendom in Europe brought with it the idea of *geographical domain*—territory being divided up into parishes and dioceses, each under the control of a monarchical ruler (priest or bishop). Within this framework, the clergy were assumed to hold spiritual authority (and sometimes a fair amount of "temporal" authority too) over everyone within their domain. Positively, this fostered the unity of a Christian society and challenged the church to attend to the spiritual needs and hopes of all the people in a given area. The medieval practice of rogation days, when the clergy would lead the members of a parish around the parish boundaries in a procession of prayer for a good harvest and for the well-being of all within the area, embodies this ideal.

One of the primary downsides is the restriction of ministry primarily to the clergy as a caste set apart and above everyone else. Two important theological and philosophical assumptions are at work here. The first is a monarchical view of Christ. During the Middle

Ages, Jesus came to be seen in the Western tradition as a powerful ruler and lord governing life on earth and in heaven. It is not uncommon to find images of Jesus as a solemn judge in medieval cathedrals. (The cult of Mary arose in part to soften this image of God.) In the Western church, there was less imagination for the Trinity as a relational community or for the leadership of the Spirit in the church's life. The second factor was a hierarchical understanding of the cosmos inherited from Greek philosophy, whereby the social order on earth reflected a divine stratification. Up through the time of the English Reformation and into the early modern period, it was assumed in Europe that social and religious hierarchy was divinely sanctioned. The hierarchical organization of the Episcopal Church today continues to embody these assumptions.

The organization of the Episcopal Church in the late eighteenth century embraced new Enlightenment ideas of democratic equality and participation. Much of the old premodern organizational DNA continued to shape the church's life, however. High-church northern leaders like Samuel Seabury, the first bishop of Connecticut, sought to retain a more clerical and hierarchical approach to church governance than William White and others from the southern and mid-Atlantic regions who wanted greater lay participation.[4] The eighteenth-century compromise that successfully provided church unity never achieved a deep or coherent integration of these tensions, and they remain alive today.

> Today, *every* congregation should be a mission congregation, and all bishops should be missionary bishops.

. American denominations were organized in the nineteenth century largely as voluntary societies to do mission somewhere else— across the frontier or overseas.[5] This reflects the establishment logic that mission is the geographical expansion of the domain of Christendom. Episcopal polity to this day preserves this view in the distinction between "parishes" and "missions" as well as between "bishops" and "missionary bishops." The Christendom unit of the "parish" is assumed to be normative, and a "mission" congregation is the exception. Likewise, "missionary bishops" are expected to graduate to "normal" status (and lose the "missionary" prefix) once a diocese is self-supporting. Establishment assumptions are deeply embedded here. Today, *every* congregation should be a mission congregation, and all bishops should be missionary bishops.

Modern Corporate Bureaucracy

presiding Bishop

In the first half of the twentieth century, the Episcopal Church and other mainline denominations embraced a form of organization on the rise within American culture—modern corporate bureaucracy. As the Episcopal Church's sense of self-confidence and centrality within American life peaked, it consolidated and expanded its program and administrative functions with a new headquarters at 815 Second Avenue, New York City, which opened in 1960. The role of presiding bishop became a full-time job, and Henry Knox Sherrill likened his position to that of the chief executive officer of a multinational corporation.[6]

The organizational paradigm of modern corporate bureaucracies contains many embedded assumptions. Modern bureaucracies assume a universe of linearity, predictability, and command-and-control. They were created during the Industrial Revolution as a means of rationalizing work.[7] Expertise is assumed to lie at the top of the organizational pyramid. The organization is designed to control the efficiency of workers at the bottom of that pyramid, who are expected to implement the commands sent from above. If there is a functioning view of God at all within the modern corporate bureaucratic paradigm, it is Deism. In Deism, God is an aloof, impersonal force who winds up the universe like a big mechanical clock and sets it in motion without subsequent interference. Humanity's job is to figure out the natural laws embedded in the cosmos and adhere to them.

The Episcopal Church's embrace of the modern corporate bureaucratic form of organization fit in many ways the early- to mid-twentieth-century U.S. context. American life was being increasingly shaped by new efforts at modernization and standardization, symbolized by large industrial corporations. For the church, this meant attempts to standardize clergy training and credentialing and to create shared Sunday school curricula and other programs. Committees, commissions, boards, and staff grew markedly at the national level as a reflection of the increased scope of the denomination's work, which included building the organizational structure of the Anglican Communion.[8]

In this era, clergy came to inhabit a new professionalized identity. As described by H. Richard Niebuhr in his study of the postwar years, clergy were "pastoral directors" of complex nonprofit voluntary organizations, serving as administrators and executives of congregations busy with programs and activities.[9] Within the modern bureaucratic paradigm, clergy were understood to function like interchangeable parts within the denominational machine, capable of ministering effectively in any context to which they might be sent. They were to be accredited professionals (like lawyers or accountants) who could expect a middle-class salary and benefits. The growth of new suburban churches in the postwar period proceeded in a franchise model. Relatively standardized churches were designed with the assumption of supporting a full-time priest and a small staff in a dedicated church building.

Denominational Systems under Stress

In the mid- to late-1960s, the modern corporate bureaucratic form of denominational organization began to come under major strain amidst dramatic cultural change, a decay of institutional loyalty, and grassroots resistance.[10] The response from American denominations followed the classic logic of a bureaucracy—trying to reassert control.

In the face of challenges to their purpose, identity, and unity, denominations began to function increasingly like regulatory agencies. For instance, ordination processes became highly complex, regulated affairs involving committees, many layers of paperwork, national exams, and multiple forms of mandatory screening for candidates. The more elaborate and expensive this process became, the more invested ordinands became in securing a full-time job with benefits at the end of it, even as those jobs began to disappear.

> Congregations want to be linked in mission, but not in the top-down, centralized ways that characterized the twentieth-century corporate bureaucratic paradigm.

Meanwhile, there developed a growing disconnect between the grassroots membership of the mainline churches and the actions of denominational staff and assemblies. In the Episcopal Church, this was well documented in an Episcopal Church Foundation study at the turn of the millennium, the Zacchaeus Project.[11] That study uncovered a renewed focus and energy for local mission carried out primarily through congregations, rather than the mission "over there" that denominational structures in America were largely designed for. The Zacchaeus Project found that congregations wanted to be linked in mission, but not in the top-down, centralized ways that characterized the twentieth-century corporate bureaucratic paradigm. Top-down attempts to dictate policy and control church life have increasingly been met with resistance, indifference, or resentment by local churches.[12]

Moreover, most existing denominational and regional judicatory structures (like dioceses) emerged out of a culture of duty and obligation, where people willingly gave money to support the church's mission somewhere else. The trust that fueled this giving has eroded. For the baby boomer and younger generations, a culture of discretion, or choice, has replaced a culture of duty and obligation. Funding is declining precipitously for diocesan and churchwide denominational budgets, and that trend will likely accelerate.

Congregational Life in the Establishment Era

Within the paradigm of establishment, congregational life was largely organized around the care of existing members. This care was typically assumed to be carried out by paid professional clergy and staff, who would design and lead the programs, worship, pastoral care, and other services that congregation members expected. In the late-modern establishment approach to congregations, a minority of staff and volunteers (typically 20 percent) provides the religious goods and services consumed by the other 80 percent.

After World War II, there was a significant increase in volunteer programs and activities in American churches. This stemmed in part from the generation of women who had stepped in to work during the war but whose factory jobs were handed over to returning men. Many turned their considerable energy and expertise toward volunteerism, including through the church. As churches were planted in the rapidly growing suburbs in the 1950s and early 60s, committees, auxiliaries, and programs abounded, altering the shape of congregational life. As the Episcopal priest Gibson Winter pointed out in his 1961 book, *The Suburban Captivity of the Churches*, this had the ironic effect of taking Christians out of the city as they grew busy with the internal life of the church.[13]

Christian discipleship came to be equated with service on church committees or attendance at church programs. The more devout you were, the more committees you sat on and the more frequently you were on the church campus. The logic of establishment is obvious here, with the church campus and its activities being seen as consecrated and implicitly holier than daily life in the neighborhood or city. Some Episcopalians took a very different path through their active involvement in political struggles for civil rights and other social justice causes. Yet the program paradigm remained predominant in many churches. It is now rapidly fading as the World War II generation that sustained the committee life of many congregations ages and younger generations are choosing to participate differently. In many families, both spouses/partners now work outside the home. Those who do have jobs in today's economy are working harder to keep them as productivity rises with a smaller workforce. It is impractical for many families to return to the church campus during the week. Institutional identity as defined through committee membership and program participation has lost its allure.

In the latter half of the twentieth century, the professional paradigm for clergy identity took on some new forms.[14] First was the *counselor* who tended to the private spiritual needs of individuals as a kind of therapist, which arose in the 1960s and 70s. Next came the *manager* or *entrepreneur* in the 1980s who was supposed to catalyze organizational renewal by bringing a dynamic vision and aligning the church around it, often through attractional marketing or programmatic strategies. Finally in the 1990s the clergyperson as *technician* came to the fore as the implementer of the latest program, technique, or seminar method for church growth, health, or renewal. These approaches are all deeply captive to the assumptions of modernity—that *aul vocation.*

faith is a private matter of individual choice, rather than a public concern; that church renewal can be managed or controlled through our own efforts; and that there are easy solutions to apply to the massive challenges of church life after establishment, rather than the hard spiritual work of wandering in the biblical wilderness or being displaced into exile until we rediscover what it means to be God's people.

Organizing for Mission

This book has asserted that renewing the church's identity involves going deep into God's Trinitarian life to recognize that the church is a product of and participant in God's reconciliation of all creation. The shape of God's communal life with and for the world must define the shape of the church's life with and for the world in God's image. In saying this, I recognize full well the limits of correlating the church's life with God's life and mission. As a human organization, the church will always be imperfect, broken, and flawed, distorting God's image in various ways. Thankfully, the vitality and effectiveness of our identity does not depend upon our ability to imitate God perfectly. Throughout the biblical story, God chooses to work through very imperfect people to further God's purposes, including a conflict-ridden (but Spirit-filled) early church. Our calling is to discern how we might faithfully share in God's renewing movement in our neighborhoods and world according to the gifts God has given us, in the power of the Spirit, *with* our very humanity. Reconciliation and salvation are God's work in, through, and beyond us—not our task to accomplish on God's behalf.

We've explored the shape of God's communal life in the Trinity, a life of mutuality, reciprocity, generosity, openness, and shared leadership. We've reflected upon God's full participation in human life in the incarnation and Jesus' self-giving, boundary-crossing ministry. This ministry reached its climax in the crucifixion, the ultimate act of vulnerable identification and loving service, and resurrection, the tangible promise of empowerment, healing, and eternal life for all who trust in it. We've traced the Spirit's creative and liberating work in forming and restoring community, especially in times of distress, injustice, and confusion. What does this image of God and sense of the church's identity suggest about organization for a twenty-first-century Episcopal Church?

Becoming Learning Communities

As I have argued, recovering a deeper and more robust practice of discipleship is integral to the renewal of Episcopal identity. To be a disciple is to be a learner, and church life in twenty-first-century America must focus on learning new ways of being God's people in a strange new land. We simply don't have clear answers yet to the big questions facing us. They are largely adaptive challenges, not technical problems that experts know how to solve.[15] Adaptive challenges are complex and ambiguous. They require learning and experimentation on the part of everyone, not just those in positions of authority. We learn as we go, and voices on the edges are often the ones who can see things most clearly. During periods of profound, discontinuous change like the one the church in the U.S. and other Western societies is facing now, the old patterns and habits yield diminishing returns.[16] Often, the tendency is simply to try harder, to do more with less. It is better to do less with more—to let go of the things that distract us from focusing on the main thing.

> We simply don't have clear answers yet to the big questions facing us. They are largely *adaptive challenges*, not technical problems that experts know how to solve.

As described earlier, the twentieth-century period of establishment and the corporate bureaucratic denomination placed a high priority on standardization, uniformity, and control. These things no longer serve us well. Trying to regulate ministry suppresses the very experimentation, risk, and innovation through which the Spirit brings forth a new future. The old franchise models are fading. Fewer and fewer churches will be able to support full-time, seminary-trained, "professional" clergy in the foreseeable future. The old "normal" for congregational life will become the exception as we enter a new phase of discovery, learning, and risk-taking.

Archbishop Rowan Williams calls this a "mixed economy" approach to church, where traditional "neighborhood" churches coexist alongside "network" churches that are organized very differently to reach people who would not attend a traditional church.[17] We must encourage a much wider diversity of forms of church than we have been accustomed to and recognize them as legitimate. Some of them will undoubtedly fail in their efforts to build Christian community with new populations and generations. That is a necessary part of the learning process. There should be no shame in it. In fact, those in positions of authority must encourage bold risk-taking, especially on the part of younger and diverse leaders, for the church's life to be translated into new vernaculars. Older generations have a powerful opportunity to invest in those experiments, rather than obstruct them, if the church is to have a future.

The future is already present in our midst, but we don't recognize it yet. The seeds of a new future already lie scattered among today's church. One of the most fascinating ideas to emerge in the field of organizational development in recent years is the concept of Positive Deviance.[18] Researchers tackling large, systemic problems like childhood malnutrition in Vietnamese villages or the prevalence of MRSA (antibiotic-resistant infections) in American hospitals discovered that some people in every community are positive deviants—they are exceptions to the problem while sharing the same living conditions. Rather than importing "expert" solutions from the outside and trying to convert local people to them, the researchers instead invited local leaders to study and learn from the positive deviants in their midst. By trying out what these community members were doing differently, lasting solutions to thorny problems began to spread.

There has been a tendency in the modern period to favor flashy, programmatic solutions to the church's challenges. Leaders look to "successful" churches, typically operating under very different conditions, and try to apply their techniques. Or strategic plans are developed that identify the congregation's deficiencies and try to close the gap through top-down, managerial methods. Typically these end up leaving people feeling shamed and blamed, with few lasting changes.[19] We can all think of strategic plans that are collecting dust on church shelves rather than facilitating real transformation.

Build upon what we have.

Instead, we might learn from approaches like Positive Deviance, Appreciative Inquiry, asset-mapping, or other community-based processes that empower local members to identify what is, in fact, working well and build upon it.[20] This affirms the contextual, incarnational character of the church—it must take root within the particularity of local cultures. In an increasingly diverse America, what allows one church to flourish in engaging its neighbors to build community may not work for another church, even within the same city. As we review the growth and development of the church in the book of Acts, we do not see big strategic plans or command-and-control methods. Rather, we see a community of learners pushed by the Spirit into engagement with their neighbors, sometimes uncomfortably, mostly improvisationally, dealing with conflict as they go. The Spirit unfolds the church's future through tangible experiences and dreams, and the disciples adapt and change every step along the way.

yes

Network Churches in a Participatory Age

The modern corporate bureaucratic form of church organization no longer serves the church well, not just because it carries deep establishment assumptions; it also doesn't fit with today's emerging participatory network culture.[21] The Internet is the primary cultural metaphor for the twenty-first-century world. It is decentralized, diverse, highly participatory, constantly evolving, and fundamentally uncontrollable. Unlike the classic bureaucratic pyramid organization, expertise and authority are distributed throughout network organizations, not just at the top. Innovation and change take place as participants adapt to local challenges. Those discoveries can be shared freely and efficiently through the network. Instead of communication being controlled by central authorities, it spreads virally on a peer-to-peer basis.[22]

> The modern corporate bureaucratic form of church organization no longer serves the church well. It doesn't fit with today's emerging participatory network culture.

This is a very different organizational paradigm than the church has been accustomed to. Yet it embodies more deeply the theological

The spirit unfolds the church's future

vision at the heart of our tradition—of a communal God whose engagement with the world is creative, dynamic, reciprocal, and participatory. One of the deep commitments within current Episcopal polity is the idea of distributed authority—that leadership in the church is shared among all four orders of ministry (lay people, bishops, priests, and deacons) through democratic processes. The Trinity is the original community of distributed authority. Networks embody the principle of shared authority much more powerfully than corporate bureaucratic organizations.

Networks are based on relationships of difference, often across social lines. Because they do not insist upon uniformity in order to be in relationship, networks can encourage the kind of reconciled diversity integral to the church's identity. They provide powerful ways for grassroots expertise to be cultivated and shared as people participate as meaningful collaborators, not passive consumers.

Network organizations have their limitations, too. Just as it is easy for people to opt in to a network, they can easily opt out. Networks can foster the kind of fickle and shifting affiliations that characterize so many relationships in contemporary culture. Unity can become frayed because it is more difficult to control those who would undermine the organization's integrity. Authority functions very differently, in a much more communal fashion, which presents a major challenge to those in formal leadership roles who are accustomed to top-down approaches. Within a network, identity must be cultivated intentionally, but not through enforcement. Rather, it takes place largely through *interpretive* leadership, helping people make sense and meaning out of what is taking place.[23] Interpretive leadership means connecting the community's stories with the biblical story and the stories of the Christian tradition.

Rethinking Ministry

Rethinking the Ministry of Lay Persons

The Book of Common Prayer states that the ministers of the church are "lay persons, bishops, priests, and deacons."[24] It is not accidental that lay persons lead the list. In the establishment mode, ministry was seen as largely confined to clergy, church volunteers, and church activities and programs. Today's new apostolic era calls us back to a much more expansive view, where every member is a missionary in daily life.[25] As the Prayer Book goes on to assert, "The ministry of lay persons is to represent Christ and his Church; to bear witness to him wherever they may be; and, according to the gifts given them, to carry on Christ's work of reconciliation in the world; and to take their place in the life, worship, and governance of the Church" (p. 855). For the most part, churches have not been organized around supporting the ministry of lay disciples in daily life. The focus has instead been church-centric—on what lay people can do to sustain the church's institutional ministry (typically through giving "time, talent, and treasure"), not on what the church can do to sustain and nourish lay disciples' ministries in the world, which is where God primarily needs them.

> If lay disciples are the primary ministers, then the church's life must be reorganized around equipping them for faithful service and witness in their spheres of influence.

This has fostered a sense of disconnection between what lay disciples face in their workplaces, homes, and neighborhoods and the church's conversation, priorities, and activities. The church has often not effectively helped cultivate a Christian theological imagination (or faithful way of seeing) among its membership that allows them to interpret God's presence and movement in daily life. A new priority must be placed on cultivating Christian practices in accessible and meaningful ways among all members. If lay disciples are in fact the primary ministers of the church, then the church's life must be reorganized around equipping them for faithful service and witness in their spheres of influence.

Rethinking the Ministry of Priests

Priests find a new role in a postestablishment world. Rather than primarily seeking to administer a nonprofit voluntary organization focused on providing religious goods and services to its members, clergy must have as their primary responsibility the cultivation of

Christian community. This includes creating spaces where lay disciples can learn the Christian story and engage it imaginatively; experience and appropriate Christian practices to nourish their own daily spiritual growth; share the deep questions and struggles they face in living as Christians in their daily lives without judgment or shame; and serve alongside one another in tending the life of the community and developing relationships with neighbors and strangers in the name of Christ.

By nature of their theological education, gifts, and role in the community, clergy have a critical part to play as interpretive leaders who help people make spiritual sense out of their lives. Rather than being experts who interpret *on behalf of* lay disciples, clergy should use their expertise in the Christian tradition to create the spaces and practices where meaningful theological interpretation and spiritual growth can take place *among* the membership. Clergy are not experts at how to live a faithful Christian witness as a nurse in a burn unit, or a corporate executive, or an immigration official, or a migrant worker, for instance. Each of those persons faces difficulties and questions clergy cannot even imagine. Yet clergy do have a pivotal role in coming alongside those disciples and helping to open up the richness of the biblical story and the wisdom of the tradition in meaningful ways. They have the charge of focusing the community's energy and conversation on what is really important. They can help the community ask the right questions, even and especially when the answers aren't clearly evident.

> Rather than being experts who interpret *on behalf of* lay disciples, clergy should use their expertise to create the spaces where meaningful theological interpretation and spiritual growth can take place *among* the membership.

This constitutes for many clergy a significant shift. Currently, many clergy feel the weight of trying to sustain institutional expectations that *they* will galvanize church growth and renewal while simultaneously taking care of all the members and avoiding the tripwires of church conflict. Many are burdened by administrative and operational responsibilities for which they are not particularly well gifted or trained. When the church is in decline, they can feel paralyzed by the erosion of institutional life amidst massive cultural change. Or when things seem to be going well and people are happy because programs and activities led and executed by clergy are popular, it can be difficult to give up this sense of success in order to change the conversation.

The kind of leadership necessary today to guide the church through this period of exile does not require high levels of charisma, heroic self-confidence, or shiny new ideas gained from the latest seminar. In fact, all of those things can be quite distracting. What is needed is the humility and posture of a learner, deep rootedness in the Christian tradition, prayerful curiosity about what God is up to in the lives of the people and in the wider neighborhood, and a capacity to convene communal practices and conversations. This means that clergy must themselves be active disciples of Jesus engaged in regular spiritual practices. Unfortunately, the late-modern establishment paradigm of church has tended to interfere with this for many clergy. They find their time fragmented by countless demands they feel they must react to; they feel the stress of trying to save the institution; they are harried by trying to take care of everyone. Often, they pray primarily when leading a prayer group, or read the Bible only when preparing a sermon or class. The church expects them to be people of deep faith, prayer, and discipleship—but often on their own time, which is already compromised by overwork.

For clergy to lead through this transition, they must share the work. The more that the church's life and ministry can be undertaken by people with particular gifts in various areas, rather than monopolized by the few, the better. Clergypersons must ask themselves, *what am I doing that someone else can do, so that I can be freed up to do what God needs me particularly to do in this place?* As long as clergy are worried and distracted by many things, the church will likely remain worried and distracted, missing the "one thing" that Jesus invites us to attend to (Luke 10:42). Rather than feeling the weight of bringing the energy to sustain everything on their own, clergy can recognize Jesus's companionship in sharing the yoke. They can trace the flow of the Spirit's energy within the life of the community, help to name it, and seek to join up with it.

Rethinking the Ministry of Bishops

The modern corporate bureaucratic form of denominational life has placed a great deal of stress on bishops, who are expected to be corporate executives who catalyze renewal and set direction for a shrinking enterprise while also providing pastoral care and inspiration to their clergy and managing a staff. They often find themselves spending significant amounts of time dealing with the legal and pastoral implications of clergy misconduct and the disposal of church property. What local priests feel in terms of institutional responsibility is often multiplied for bishops, combined with the expectation that they will serve on a dozen or more institutional boards and participate in denomination-wide and Anglican Communion commissions and committees.

Much of this serves as a distraction from the pressing adaptive challenges that bishops must focus the church's attention on. Like local priests, bishops might fruitfully reconceive their roles as theological interpreters and cultivators of spaces of discernment for mission. In the establishment paradigm, it was assumed that local churches would serve the greater mission of the diocese (primarily through sending financial support). That was because mission was understood to take place primarily somewhere other than through local churches. The logic must now be reversed. If local churches are the primary centers of mission, the diocese is the means of networking those churches and other ministries into a vibrant and collaborative whole.

> Bishops should encourage innovation and discovery in mission, using their role to convene spaces of storytelling and learning where what God is innovating at the grass roots can be shared by all.

The cultivation work of bishops and their staff thus occurs primarily across congregational boundaries as they help to link churches together, not through regulation and control, but through mutual partnerships. Bishops must become network hubs and facilitators. Within networks, communication is vital, and it must be carefully developed. Bishops and other diocesan-level leaders have opportunities to create the structures and means by which fruitful communication, sharing, and collaboration can take place among grassroots disciples and communities. Some dioceses have recently tried to shift from a regulatory to a resourcing paradigm.[26] However, this doesn't go far enough. It still assumes that missionary expertise primarily lies within diocesan or denominational staff and structures, rather than at the grass roots. A more radically decentralized peer-to-peer network structure affirms the reality that innovation and expertise in mission are primarily local, rooted at the congregational level. It seeks to share that innovation and expertise by meaningfully connecting local churches together.

Just like lay disciples and priests, bishops must recognize how crucial the vibrancy of their own practice of discipleship is to the life and witness of the church. Bishops are called to represent the depth of the Christian tradition as symbols of the unity and catholicity (universality) of the church. They have the sacred trust to be mediators of that tradition as they interpret and open it up for new generations and populations. Rather than being monarchical controllers of fiefdoms or top-down corporate regulators, bishops should encourage innovation and discovery in mission, using their role to convene spaces of storytelling and learning where what God is innovating at the grass roots can be shared by all.

Rethinking the Ministry of Deacons

The recovery of the real (vs. "transitional") diaconate within the Episcopal Church and several other mainline denominations within recent decades is a promising development that invites further consideration. Deacons in the early church were emissaries entrusted with a sacred commission across boundaries. They held executive authority and were responsible for the proclamation of the gospel, working closely with bishops as administrators of ministry in large areas.[27] We need diaconal leadership in today's new apostolic era, particularly in fostering partnerships between local ministry teams, congregations, community leaders, and civil society organizations.

The ordination liturgy for deacons in the Book of Common Prayer speaks of the vital role that deacons have in interpreting the needs, concerns, and hopes of the world to the church.[28] Deacons can play an essential part in helping the church reflect upon the realities of its local context through guiding members in studying the neighborhood

a deacon for every church

or surrounding area, identifying ministry needs and opportunities, and coordinating responses. Because they work on the regional level, they have the ability to facilitate the kind of creative mission efforts that link local churches with their surrounding neighborhoods and lead those churches into service there.

As the diaconate is being renewed in many dioceses, it may be re-interpreted for a postestablishment missionary context.[29] Rather than primarily being construed as a ministry of care-giving service, the diaconate can be understood in a more apostolic vein. Deacons can offer crucial leadership in interfacing with new populations and gen-erations. They can lead "plunging" teams. Many churches need help in developing community with underserved groups. Deacons can be pivotal bridge-builders within and across congregations in relation-ship to those not yet part of the church.

Rethinking Church Conventions

When the church gathers in representative assemblies at the diocesan and denominational levels, the primary focus today is typically on legislation. While it is necessary for some policy and governance deci-sions to be made in these conventions, this emphasis is a holdover of the establishment paradigm. A great deal of energy is spent in politi-cal maneuvering and debate, and cultural differences in the church inevitably surface in divisive ways. Those who hold minority views are often disenfranchised by the process.

It would be more fruitful for conventions at the diocesan and churchwide levels to be reconceived as missionary convocations dedicated to sharing grassroots innovation. Rather than a top-down approach, these gatherings could be designed in an open-source, par-ticipatory manner where people across the church or across a diocese could learn what the Spirit is innovating in various contexts, network for peer-to-peer sharing, and have their imaginations inspired and encouraged by new possibilities in mission.

This kind of peer-to-peer sharing could also fruitfully take place through the Internet or other kinds of networked gatherings. The Fresh Expressions movement in the UK is an excellent example within Anglicanism of a network organization that is fostering creativity and innovation through its web and training resources.[30] This kind of networking must become the primary focus for denominational and diocesan organizations in a missionary era.

Conclusion

Organizational change for the church is often painful and slow. Within the framework of establishment, the church has tended by nature to be conservative in its organizational life—trying to preserve and maintain what it has. This is understandable and in some ways commendable. The church's treasures are precious, and they must be stewarded well. Like other churches of the Reformation, the Episcopal Church's focus has tended to look backward, toward earlier patterns and practices in Christian history. This is a necessary and important turn—the church is always *reforming*. At the same time, we've lost sight of the fact that the church is always also *forming*—innovating new ways of creating Christian community under the Spirit's leadership.[31] Now is a moment in which to shift our focus to discerning what new life the Spirit of God wants to bring forth in our midst. This means making space for new expressions of church within existing structures. It invites us to suspend current rules and regulations until new and more adequate patterns emerge. It calls us to prioritize learning and discovery over maintenance and control. Given the accelerating trends of institutional decline facing the Episcopal Church and other mainline denominations in the U.S., many structures will not last very long in their current configurations. We have the choice of whether to recognize the death and rebirth of these structures and patterns as integral to the church's process of dying and rising in Christ, or to pour our energy into resistance, which will not likely change the outcome anyway.

When I joined the staff of St. David's Episcopal Church in Ashburn, Virginia, a decade ago, I had the opportunity to help develop a twenty-first-century local church ministry structure. The founding rector had cultivated a pioneer ethos of risk-taking and innovation. With the bishop's support, there was freedom to experiment with new forms of organization. We began by taking seriously the gifts and passions of lay disciples in our midst. They were the ones who had the greatest expertise about how to be in mission in that place.

For instance, Dee, a county social worker, was a natural mentor to teengers and young families. She became central to the church's newcomer ministry and coordinated the teams involved in worship. Stacy grew in her spiritual and vocational depth as she came to oversee a thriving lay pastoral care ministry. She eventually transitioned from her airline job to the church staff, taking additional responsibility for leadership development. Jim, a recently-retired businessman with a military background, accepted a call to become the church's general manager, leading and overseeing the property, finance, and preschool staff. "Pastoral" is probably the last word Jim would use to describe himself. Yet I witnessed him patiently and gently offering wise counsel to staff and congregation members day after day in his office. He did all this without taking a salary. When he did decide to reenter the workforce in another organization for a while, it was on the condition that his outside salary be donated to the church.

These leaders at St. David's were focused on equipping the congregation to live more deeply into the Christian life and to share that life with others in the world. They are examples of the power unleashed when disciples are freed to serve with their gifts in ministry. There are countless Episcopalians who have enormous gifts to offer the church as it participates in God's mission. Too often, those gifts remain undiscovered and underutilized. Helping people to hear God's call, discern how God has shaped them for ministry, and share in the church's life and leadership is critical. Like most churches, St. David's faced many challenges. There are no easy solutions to being church in a postestablishment world. Yet opening up space to innovate and adapt, to call forth the gifts among all of God's people, creates the possibility of a more vibrant and faithful future.

> Opening up space to innovate and adapt, to call forth the gifts among all of God's people, creates the possibility of a more vibrant and faithful future.

I pray that across the church, we are able to recognize that God is profoundly present in the very midst of the challenges and changes facing us—that the church's very life exists within the triune God's ongoing movement in the world. I hope that we will find the grace and wisdom of Mary to sit at Jesus' feet long enough to change our ways of seeing and be freed from our many distractions. I dream that ordinary disciples will be encouraged, supported, and empowered in the Christian habits and practices that allow them to live more deeply into their identity as people of the Way. I yearn for a new willingness to risk relying upon the hospitality of our neighbors as relationships are cultivated and stories shared. I pray that we might go forth with Christ to those people in our communities seeking meaning, purpose, hope, healing, justice, and community, as I was so many years ago in a California beach town. There are many, many others like me. I hope that in our encounters with them, we may experience and share tangible expressions of God's reconciliation of the world, because that is where our identity lies.

Questions for Discussion

1. How might your church better support your ministry in daily life?

2. What seeds of a new future might be present within your congregation's life? How might you discover them?

3. Many gifts are needed for the innovation of new forms of church in our day. What do you personally feel called to contribute?

4. How do you envision the transformation of the structures of church life to support mission in this new apostolic era?

our identity lies in sharing tangible expressions of God's reconciliation of the world

Notes

Foreword

1. I appreciate that the Episcopal Church is, in fact, a multinational church with dioceses and churches in Asia, Latin America, the Caribbean, and Europe. The primary audience of this book, however, is Episcopalians in the United States and so the Foreword will speak more to the experience of the church in the United States.

2. "Comparative Statistics of the Episcopal Church, U.S.A." *The Episcopal Church Annual, 2010* (Harrisburg: Morehouse, 2010), 20–21.

3. From page 3 of the Introduction.

Introduction

1. Throughout this book, I will use the terms "Anglican" and "Episcopal." Anglican refers to the larger communion of churches with historic roots in the Church of England, of which the Episcopal Church is one. "Anglican" in this book is meant to refer expansively to the multiple expressions of contemporary Anglican churches in the U.S., including the Episcopal Church. I do not intend it to refer more narrowly to churches that have broken away from the Episcopal Church.

2. See chapter 2 for a more detailed discussion of these trends.

3. For further discussion of the limitations of church-centric approaches, see Darrell L. Guder, ed., *Missional Church: A Vision for the Sending of the Church in North America* (Grand Rapids, MI: W. B. Eerdmans, 1998); Alan J. Roxburgh, *Missional: Joining God in the Neighborhood* (Grand Rapids, MI: Baker Books, 2011); and Craig Van Gelder and Dwight Zscheile, *The Missional Church in Perspective: Mapping Trends and Shaping the Conversation* (Grand Rapids, MI: Baker Academic, 2011).

4. See Acts 19:9, 22:4, 24:14.

5. See Rodney Stark, *The Rise of Christianity: A Sociologist Reconsiders History* (Princeton, NJ: Princeton University Press, 1996).

6. See, for instance, Stephen Sykes, *The Integrity of Anglicanism* (New York: Seabury Press, 1978), and Paul D. L. Avis, *The Identity of Anglicanism: Essentials of Anglican Ecclesiology* (New York: T & T Clark, 2007).

7. See Henry Luke Orombi, "What Is Anglicanism?" *First Things* 175 (August 1, 2007): 23–28; and Ian T. Douglas, "Inculturation and Anglican Worship," in *The Oxford Guide to the Book of Common Prayer*, ed. Charles Hefling and Cynthia Shattuck (New York: Oxford University Press, 2006), 271–76.

8. See http://fca.net/resources/the_jerusalem_declaration/.

9. Interim Report of the House of Deputies Committee on the State of the Church, November 2007.

10. David T. Gortner, "Around One Table: Exploring Episcopal Identity" (online, College for Bishops/CREDO Institute, 2009).

11. The system-wide participatory action research process was the focus of my doctoral dissertation, "Reframing Mission: An Action-Research Intervention into a Mainline Judicatory" (unpublished PhD dissertation, Luther Seminary, St. Paul, 2008). The identity of the diocese shall go unnamed to protect the anonymity of those involved.

12. "Inclusion" is among the top ten themes cited in the Episcopal Identity Project. See "Around One Table," 28.

13. This diocese was hardly atypical in its need for spiritual revitalization. The 2010 Faith Communities Today Survey found that only 28 percent of Episcopal churches reported high spiritual vitality. See David A. Roozen, "A Decade of Change in American Congregations 2000–2010" (Hartford, CT: Hartford Institute for Religion Research, 2011), 17.

14. For a recent study of young adults, see David Kinnaman and Aly Hawkins, *You Lost Me: Why Young Christians Are Leaving Church . . . and Rethinking Faith* (Grand Rapids, MI: Baker Books, 2011).

15. "Episcopal Domestic Fast Facts: 2010," www.episcopalchurch.org.

Chapter One

1. I am indebted to Brian McLaren for his use of a similar image to describe the church's predicament.

2. See Ephesians 4, 1 Corinthians 12, and Romans 12, for instance, and James Tunstead Burtchaell, *From Synagogue to Church: Public Services and Offices in the Earliest Christian Communities* (New York: Cambridge University Press, 1992).

3. Robert W. Prichard, *A History of the Episcopal Church*, rev. ed. (Harrisburg, PA: Morehouse Pub., 1999), 9–10. In the northern colonies, there was a more clerical approach to leadership.

4. Ibid., 73–79.

5. Ian T. Douglas, *Fling Out the Banner!: The National Church Ideal and the Foreign Mission of the Episcopal Church* (New York: Church Hymnal Corp., 1996), 27–35.

6. David Hein and Gardiner H. Shattuck, *The Episcopalians* (Westport, CT: Praeger Publishers, 2004), 69.

7. Kit Konolige and Frederica Konolige, *The Power of Their Glory: America's Ruling Class: The Episcopalians* (New York: Wyden Books, 1978).

8. These surveys were repeated in 2010 and found comparable results. See David Leonhardt, "Is Your Religion Your Financial Destiny?" *New York Times Magazine*, May 15, 2011.

9. See Douglas, *Banner*, and Frank Sugeno, "The Establishmentarian Ideal and the Mission of the Episcopal Church," *Historical Magazine of the Protestant Episcopal Church* 53, no. 4 (December 1984), 285–92.

10. Sydney E. Ahlstrom, *A Religious History of the American People* (New Haven, CT: Yale University Press, 1972), 630.

11. Douglas, *Banner*, 88–89.

12. Ibid., 91.

13. Ibid., 94.

14. Ibid., 31–32.

15. See Frederick W. Danker, *Benefactor: Epigraphic Study of a Graeco-Roman and New Testament Semantic Field* (St. Louis: Clayton Publishing House, 1982).

16. See Douglas, *Banner*, 289–93.

17. See Gardiner H. Shattuck, *Episcopalians and Race: Civil War to Civil Rights* (Lexington, KY: University Press of Kentucky, 2000).

18. See, for example, Shattuck, *Episcopalians and Race*, and Juan M. C. Oliver, *Ripe Fields: The Promise and Challenge of Latino Ministry* (New York: Church Publishing, 2009).

19. For further discussion of this political impulse, see James Davison Hunter, *To Change the World: The Irony, Tragedy, and Possibility of Christianity in the Late Modern World* (New York: Oxford University Press, 2010).

20. See David Kinnaman and Gabe Lyons, *Unchristian: What a New Generation Really Thinks About Christianity—and Why It Matters* (Grand Rapids, MI: Baker Books, 2007). Much of the negativity is toward right-wing political activism, but left-wing activism actually shares many basic assumptions.

21. See Michel de Certeau, *The Practice of Everyday Life* (Berkeley: University of California Press, 1984), 35–38.

22. "Episcopal Domestic Fast Facts: 2010," www.episcopalchurch.org.

23. Kirk Hadaway, "Episcopal Congregations Overview: Findings from the 2010 Faith Communities Today Survey" (New York: Episcopal Church Center, 2011).

Chapter Two

1. See Patricia O'Connell Killen and Mark Silk, *Religion and Public Life in the Pacific Northwest: The None Zone* (Walnut Creek, CA: AltaMira Press, 2004).

2. 2008 U.S. General Social Survey. Association of Religion Data Archives, www.thearda.com, accessed June 24, 2010.

3. David T. Olson, *The American Church in Crisis* (Grand Rapids, MI: Zondervan, 2008), 29. Only 3 percent of the population was in mainline Protestant churches. It should be noted that the percentage of Americans who *claim* to attend church weekly has hovered around 40 percent for several decades.

4. Baylor Religion Survey, Wave 2, 2007, www.thearda.com, accessed June 8, 2011.

5. Robert Wuthnow, *After the Baby Boomers: How Twenty- and Thirty-Somethings Are Shaping the Future of American Religion* (Princeton, NJ: Princeton University Press, 2007), 76.

6. Christian Smith and Melinda Lundquist Denton, *Soul Searching: The Religious and Spiritual Lives of American Teenagers* (New York: Oxford University Press, 2005), 162–63.

7. Ibid., 165.

8. Alan Wolfe, *The Transformation of American Religion: How We Actually Live Our Faith* (New York: Free Press, 2003), 36.

9. Smith and Denton, *Soul Searching*, 133.

10. Wolfe, *Transformation*, 247.

11. Christian Smith with Patricia Snell, *Souls in Transition: The Religious and Spiritual Lives of Emerging Adults* (New York: Oxford University Press, 2009), 116.

12. Wuthnow, *After the Baby Boomers*, 134–35.

13. Charles Taylor, *A Secular Age* (Cambridge, MA: Belknap Press of Harvard University Press, 2007), 288.

14. Among these are various forms of Pietism, evangelicalism, revivalistic Christianity, Romanticism, and Pentecostalism, which have asserted an active spiritual presence in the cosmos. It should be noted that this secularism has been strongest in the dominant white culture, while many other cultures have been more resistant to it.

15. Taylor, *A Secular Age*, 299.

16. Wuthnow, *After the Baby Boomers*, 21–23.

17. Anthony Giddens, *The Transformation of Intimacy: Sexuality, Love, and Eroticism in Modern Societies* (Stanford, CA: Stanford University Press, 1992).

18. Zygmunt Bauman, *Identity* (Malden, MA: Polity Press, 2004), 13.

19. Zygmunt Bauman, *Community: Seeking Safety in an Insecure World* (Malden, MA: Polity Press, 2001), 116.

20. Bauman, *Community*, 135.

21. Jennifer M. Ortman and Christine E Guarneri, "United States Population Projections: 2000 to 2050" (Washington, DC: U.S. Census Bureau, 2009).

22. Jehu Hanciles, *Beyond Christendom: Globalization, African Migration, and the Transformation of the West* (Maryknoll, NY: Orbis Books, 2008).

23. See Lamin O. Sanneh, *Translating the Message: The Missionary Impact on Culture* (Maryknoll, NY: Orbis Books, 1989).

24. See Wayne A. Meeks, *The First Urban Christians: The Social World of the Apostle Paul* (New Haven, CT: Yale University Press, 1983).

25. For a critical appraisal of Western culture today from a Christian perspective, see Graham S. Ward, *The Politics of Discipleship: Becoming Postmaterial Citizens* (Grand Rapids, MI: Baker Academic, 2009).

26. The roots of this secularization of Christianity go deep into the early twentieth century in figures like Rudolf Bultmann, but it reached its crest in the 1960s and '70s with books like Harvey Cox's *Secular City* and has lingered on in the Episcopal Church through authors like John Shelby Spong.

Chapter Three

1. See, for instance, Matthew 3:16–17 and 28:19, 2 Corinthians 13:13, Ephesians 4:4–6.

2. The Bible includes both maternal and paternal imagery for God. Jesus referred to God often as "Father," and that became the predominant term in subsequent tradition. In this book, I will seek to be inclusive without losing the personal relationality that is so important to a Trinitarian understanding.

3. See Jürgen Moltmann, "Perichoresis: An Old Magic Word for a New Trinitarian Theology," in *Trinity, Community and Power: Mapping Trajectories in Wesleyan Theology*, ed. M. Douglas Meeks (Nashville: Kingswood Books, 2000), 111–26.

4. See John D. Zizioulas, *Communion and Otherness: Further Studies in Personhood and the Church* (New York: T & T Clark, 2007), 1–12.

5. Lesslie Newbigin, *The Open Secret: An Introduction to the Theology of Mission*, rev. ed. (Grand Rapids, MI: W. B. Eerdmans, 1995), 68–77.

6. Walter Brueggemann, *The Prophetic Imagination*, 2nd ed. (Minneapolis, MN: Fortress Press, 2001).

7. Deuteronomy 21:23.

8. See Jürgen Moltmann, *The Crucified God: The Cross of Christ as the Foundation and Criticism of Christian Theology* (Minneapolis, MN: Fortress Press, 1993), 249.

9. See Jürgen Moltmann, *The Trinity and the Kingdom: The Doctrine of God* (Minneapolis, MN: Fortress Press, 1993), 80–83.

10. For further discussion, see Andrew F. Walls, *The Missionary Movement in Christian History: Studies in the Transmission of Faith* (Maryknoll, NY: Orbis Books, 1996).

11. See Craig Van Gelder, *The Ministry of the Missional Church* (Grand Rapids, MI: Baker Academic, 2007).

12. See Lesslie Newbigin, *The Gospel in a Pluralist Society* (Grand Rapids, MI: W. B. Eerdmans, 1989), 222–33.

13. Van Gelder, *The Ministry of the Missional Church*, 56.

14. On the theme of participation in Anglican theology, see A. M. Allchin, *Participation in God: A Forgotten Strand in Anglican Tradition* (Wilton, CT: Morehouse-Barlow, 1988). Unlike many other Anglican authors, I do not use participation in the Platonic sense; for further discussion of the Platonic background, see Paul S. Fiddes, *Participating in God: A Pastoral Doctrine of the Trinity* (Louisville, KY: Westminster John Knox Press, 2000), 11–56. On mission and participation, see Jannie Swart et al., "Toward a Missional Theology of Participation," *Missiology* 37, no. 1 (January 2009): 75–87; and Van Gelder and Zscheile, *Missional Church in Perspective*, 101–23.

15. See Mark Lau Branson, *Memories, Hopes, and Conversations: Appreciative Inquiry and Congregational Change* (Herndon, VA: Alban Institute, 2004).

16. Richard Hooker and W. Speed Hill, *The Laws of Ecclesiastical Polity*, vol. 2, The Folger Library Edition of the Works of Richard Hooker (Cambridge, MA: Belknap Press of Harvard University Press, 1977), 234–48.

17. For a further discussion of the theme of *theosis* (participation or divinization) in relation to mission and spiritual formation, see Dwight Zscheile, "A Missional Theology of Spiritual Formation," in *Cultivating Sent Communities: Missional Spiritual Formation*, ed. Dwight Zscheile (Grand Rapids, MI: Eerdmans, 2012), 1–28.

Chapter Four

1. John D. Zizioulas, *Being as Communion: Studies in Personhood and the Church* (Crestwood, NY: St. Vladimir's Seminary Press, 1985), 1–65. See also

Stanley J. Grenz, *The Social God and the Relational Self: A Trinitarian Theology of the Imago Dei* (Louisville, KY: Westminster John Knox Press, 2001).

2. Sanneh, *Translating the Message*.

3. Episcopal Church, *The Book of Common Prayer* (New York: Church Hymnal Corporation and Seabury Press, 1979), 308.

4. See Patrick R. Keifert, *Welcoming the Stranger: A Public Theology of Worship and Evangelism* (Minneapolis, MN: Fortress Press, 1992).

5. Edmond L. Browning, *No Outcasts: The Public Witness of Edmond L. Browning, 24th Presiding Bishop of the Episcopal Church*, ed. Brian J. Grieves (Cincinnati, OH: Forward Movement, 1997), 24.

6. Putnam and Campbell point out that fundamentalist theological beliefs are uncorrelated with bridging of social class and argue that it is the sociology, more than the theology, of evangelical churches that fosters this. This includes the high prevalence of small group participation in evangelical churches. See Robert D. Putnam and David E. Campbell, *American Grace: How Religion Divides and Unites Us* (New York: Simon & Schuster, 2010), 254.

7. See Gary M. Simpson, *Critical Social Theory: Prophetic Reason, Civil Society, and Christian Imagination* (Minneapolis, MN: Fortress Press, 2002), 115–17.

8. John Locke, "A Letter Concerning Toleration," in *Locke on Politics, Religion, and Education*, ed. Maurice Cranston (New York: Collier, 1965), 110–11.

9. On the theme of experiential satisfaction as the predominant way of understanding human flourishing in contemporary America, see Miroslav Volf, *A Public Faith: How Followers of Christ Should Serve the Common Good* (Grand Rapids, MI: Brazos Press, 2011), 57–58.

10. See Bruce Kaye, *An Introduction to World Anglicanism* (New York: Cambridge University Press, 2008), 92.

11. The creative and innovative mission efforts unleashed in the UK by the Fresh Expressions movement are due in part to the fact that the Church of England still feels a sense of responsibility for all the residents of the nation—something the Episcopal Church largely lost with the collapse of the national church ideal. See www.freshexpressions.org.uk.

12 Jürgen Habermas has been a key voice of reclaiming the deliberative stream of democracy. See Jürgen Habermas, *The Theory of Communicative Action*, 2 vols. (Boston: Beacon Press, 1984).

13. See Simpson, *Critical Social Theory*, 134–45.

14. Classically in Christian theology, the Spirit is indicated by a masculine personal pronoun. However, just as with God the Creator, the Spirit is neither male nor female and is portrayed biblically and in the tradition in feminine terms alongside masculine ones. See Elizabeth A. Johnson, *She Who Is:*

The Mystery of God in Feminist Theological Discourse (New York: Crossroad, 1992), 124–49.

15. Michael Welker, *God the Spirit* (Minneapolis, MN: Fortress Press, 1994), 2.

16. Ibid., 21–22.

17. Ibid., 56.

18. Ibid., 124–34.

19. Ibid., 21–27.

20. See Kathryn Tanner, *Christ the Key* (New York: Cambridge University Press, 2010).

Chapter Five

1. See Patrick R. Keifert, *We Are Here Now: A New Missional Era* (Eagle, ID: Allelon, 2006), and Alan Roxburgh, *Missional: Joining God in the Neighborhood*.

2. For rich discussions of hospitality and the church, see Stephanie Spellers, *Radical Welcome: Embracing God, the Other and the Spirit of Transformation* (New York: Church Publishing, 2006), and Christine D. Pohl, *Making Room: Recovering Hospitality as a Christian Tradition* (Grand Rapids, MI: W. B. Eerdmans, 1999).

3. This text has come to play a central role in the missional transformation of churches around the world through the Partnership for Missional Church process of Church Innovations Institute, which received the text from Native American Episcopalians in Minnesota. See Keifert, *We Are Here Now*, 69.

4. Mark Chaves, *Congregations in America* (Cambridge, MA: Harvard University Press, 2004), 65.

5. Roxburgh, *Missional: Joining God in the Neighborhood*, 85–92.

6. Plunging was innovated within the framework of the Partnership for Missional Church renewal process. See Keifert, *We Are Here Now,* or www.churchinnovations.org. For a South African perspective on plunging, see Danie Mouton, "To Plunge or Not to Plunge," www.communitas.co.za/conferences/2009-to-plunge-or-not-to-plunge?lang. I am grateful to Jannie Swart, Breda Ludik, and Colin Campbell for sharing stories of plunging.

7. Mouton, "To Plunge or Not to Plunge."

8. See Elizabeth Conde-Frazier, "From Hospitality to Shalom" in Elizabeth Conde-Frazier, S. Steve Kang. and Gary Parrett, *A Many Colored Kingdom: Multicultural Dynamics for Spiritual Formation* (Grand Rapids, MI: Baker Academic, 2004), 167–210.

9. Newbigin, *The Gospel in a Pluralist Society*, 14.

10. See Volf, *A Public Faith*, 119–37.

11. Hunter, *To Change the World*, 243–54.

Chapter Six

1. *Epistle to Diognetus*, in Tim Dowley, *Eerdmans' Handbook to the History of Christianity* (Grand Rapids, MI: Eerdmans, 1977), 69.

2. Stark, *The Rise of Christianity*.

3. See Allen Hilton, "Living into the Big Story: The Missional Trajectory of Scripture in Congregational Life," in *Cultivating Sent Communities: Missional Spiritual Formation*, ed. Dwight Zscheile (Grand Rapids, MI: Eerdmans, 2012), 81–101.

4. See Keifert, *We Are Here Now*, 69–71. The "Bible in the Life of the Church" project was launched in the Anglican Communion in 2009 to address how scripture is used across different cultural contexts within Anglicanism.

5. Patrick Keifert, "The Bible and Theological Education: A Report and Reflections on a Journey," in *The Ending of Mark and the Ends of God*, ed. Beverly Roberts Gaventa and Patrick D. Miller (Louisville, KY: Westminster/John Knox, 2005), 165–82.

6. Volf, *A Public Faith*, 57–58.

7. William J. Abraham, *The Logic of Evangelism: The Creed, Spiritual Gifts, and Disciplines* (Grand Rapids, MI: W. B. Eerdmans, 1989), 95.

8. Newbigin, *The Open Secret*, 48.

9. Craig Van Gelder, *The Essence of the Church: A Community Created by the Spirit* (Grand Rapids, MI: Baker Books, 2000), 99–100.

10. See Ian T. Douglas, "Anglican Identity and the *Missio Dei*: Implications for the American Convocation of Churches in Europe," *Anglican Theological Review* 82, no. 3 (Summer 2000): 460–66.

11. Lesslie Newbigin, *Foolishness to the Greeks: The Gospel and Western Culture* (Grand Rapids, MI: W. B. Eerdmans, 1986), 4.

12. David A. Roozen and James R. Nieman, *Church, Identity, and Change: Theology and Denominational Structures in Unsettled Times* (Grand Rapids, MI: W. B. Eerdmans, 2005), 614.

13. See Robert Webber, *Evangelicals on the Canterbury Trail: Why Evangelicals Are Attracted to the Liturgical Church* (Harrisburg, PA: Morehouse Publishing, 1985).

14. Kinnaman and Hawkins, *You Lost Me*, 185–98.

15. *The Rule of St. Benedict*, trans. Anthony C. Meisel and M.L. del Mastro (New York: Image Books, 1975), 45.

16. For an example of a church that lived into this vision intentionally, see Mark Lau Branson, "Ecclesiology and Leadership for the Missional Church," in *The Missional Church in Context: Helping Congregations Develop Contextual Ministry*, ed. Craig Van Gelder (Grand Rapids, MI: W. B. Eerdmans, 2007), 94–125.

17. See Stephen B. Bevans and Roger Schroeder, *Constants in Context: A Theology of Mission for Today* (Maryknoll, NY: Orbis Books, 2004), 99–170.

18. Richard J. Foster, *Celebration of Discipline: The Path to Spiritual Growth*, rev. ed. (San Francisco: Harper & Row, 1988), 1.

19. See www.missionorder.org and Jonathan Wilson-Hartgrove, *New Monasticism: What It Has to Say to Today's Church* (Grand Rapids, MI: Brazos Press, 2008).

Chapter Seven

1. For a further discussion, see Dwight Zscheile, "A More True 'Domestic and Foreign Missionary Society': Toward a Missional Polity for the Episcopal Church," in *The Missional Church and Denominations*, ed. Craig Van Gelder (Grand Rapids, MI: W. B. Eerdmans, 2008), 133–65.

2. Richard Hooker, *Ecclesiastical Polity*, III.x.7, ed. Arthur Pollard (Manchester: Carcanet, 1990), 120.

3. William White, *The Case of the Episcopal Churches in the United States Considered* (Philadelphia: David C. Claypoole, 1782).

4. Prichard, *A History of the Episcopal Church*, 84–90.

5. For a general history of denominationalism in America, see Craig Dykstra and James Hudnut-Beumler, "The National Organizational Structures of Protestant Denominations: An Invitation to a Conversation," in *The Organizational Revolution: Presbyterians and American Denominationalism*, ed. Milton J. Coalter, John M. Mulder, and Louis Weeks (Louisville, KY: Westminster/John Knox Press, 1992), 306–30; and Russell E. Richey, "Denominations and Denominationalism: An American Morphology," in *Reimagining Denominationalism: Interpretive Essays*, ed. Robert Bruce Mullin, and Russell E. Richey (New York: Oxford University Press, 1994), 74–98. For a helpful exploration of the Episcopal version of this history, see Ian T. Douglas, "Whither the National Church? Reconsidering the Mission Structures of the Episcopal Church," in *A New Conversation: Essays on the Future of Theology and the Episcopal Church*, ed. Robert Boak Slocum (New York: Church Publishing, 1999), 60–78.

6. Douglas, *Banner*, 226.

7. For the classic exposition, see Max Weber, *The Theory of Social and Economic Organization*, ed. Talcott Parsons (New York: Free Press, [1947] 1997).

8. Douglas, *Banner*, 236–47.

9. H. Richard Niebuhr, *The Purpose of the Church and Its Ministry: Reflections on the Aims of Theological Education* (New York: Harper, 1956).

10. See Richey, "Denominations and Denominationalism" and Craig Van Gelder, "From Corporate Church to Missional Church: The Challenge Facing Congregations Today," *Review & Expositor* 101, no. 3 (2004): 425–50.

11. William L. Sachs, Thomas P. Holland, and the Episcopal Church Foundation, *Restoring the Ties That Bind: The Grassroots Transformation of the Episcopal Church* (New York: Church Publishing, 2003).

12. See Richey, "Denominations and Denominationalism," 87–90.

13. Gibson Winter, *The Suburban Captivity of the Churches: An Analysis of Protestant Responsibility in the Expanding Metropolis* (Garden City, NY: Doubleday, 1961).

14. See Alan Roxburgh, "Missional Leadership: Equipping God's People for Mission," in Guder, ed., *Missional Church: A Vision for the Sending of the Church in North America*, 196–98.

15. See Ronald A. Heifetz and Martin Linsky, *Leadership on the Line: Staying Alive through the Dangers of Leading* (Boston, MA: Harvard Business School Press, 2002).

16. See Alan J. Roxburgh and Fred Romanuk, *The Missional Leader: Equipping Your Church to Reach a Changing World* (San Francisco, CA: Jossey-Bass, 2006).

17. Rowan Williams, "Traditional and Emerging Church" (paper presented at the General Synod, York, July 14, 2003). For a rich discussion of network and neighborhood churches, see The Archbishops' Council, *Mission-Shaped Church: Church Planting and Fresh Expressions of Church in a Changing Context* (New York: Church Publishing, 2010).

18. See Richard T. Pascale, Jerry Sternin, and Monique Sternin, *The Power of Positive Deviance: How Unlikely Innovators Solve the World's Toughest Problems* (Boston: Harvard Business Press, 2010).

19. For a different approach, see Keifert, *We Are Here Now*; Roxburgh and Romanuk, *The Missional Leader*; and Everett M. Rogers, *Diffusion of Innovations*, 5th ed. (New York: Free Press, 2003).

20. There is a wide array of literature on these topics, including Peter Block, *Community: The Structure of Belonging* (San Francisco: Berrett-Koehler Publishers, 2008), and Peter M. Senge, *The Fifth Discipline: The Art and Practice of the Learning Organization* (New York: Doubleday/Currency, 1990).

21. American businesses and other organizations have already largely adapted to this shift. See, for instance, Ronald N. Ashkenas, *The Boundaryless Organization: Breaking the Chains of Organizational Structure*, 2nd ed. (San Francisco: Jossey-Bass, 2002).

22. For further discussion of networks, see Albert-Laszlo Barabasi, *Linked: How Everything Is Connected to Everything Else and What It Means for Business, Science, and Everyday Life* (New York: Plume, 2003); Clay Shirky, *Here Comes Everybody: The Power of Organizing without Organizations* (New York: Penguin Press, 2008); and Yochai Benkler, *The Wealth of Networks: How Social Production Transforms Markets and Freedom* (New Haven, CT: Yale Univer-

sity Press, 2006). For additional reflection on network organizations and their implications for the church, see Dwight Zscheile, "Social Networking and Church Systems," *Word & World* 30, no. 3 (Summer 2010): 249–57.

23. See Scott Cormode, *Making Spiritual Sense: Christian Leaders as Spiritual Interpreters* (Nashville: Abingdon Press, 2006).

24. *The Book of Common Prayer*, 855.

25. See A. Wayne Schwab, *When the Members Are the Missionaries: An Extraordinary Calling for Ordinary People* (Essex, NY: Member Mission Press, 2002).

26. A recent book that advocates this approach is J. Russell Crabtree, *The Fly in the Ointment: Why Denominations Aren't Helping Their Congregations . . . and How They Can* (New York: Church Publishing, 2008).

27. See John N. Collins, *Deacons and the Church: Making Connections between Old and New* (Harrisburg, PA: Morehouse Publishing, 2002).

28. *The Book of Common Prayer*, 543.

29. For a helpful discussion of reenvisioning Episcopal ministry, see Ian T. Douglas, "Baptized into Mission: Ministry and Holy Orders Reconsidered," *Sewanee Theological Review* 40, no. 4 (1997): 431–43.

30. See www.freshexpressions.org.uk.

31. See Van Gelder, *The Ministry of the Missional Church*, 54–56.